POTTERIES

LAD

Bill Ridgway

THE ARTICLES IN THIS BOOK ORIGINALLY
APPEARED IN THE STAFFORDSHIRE EVENING
SENTINEL PRODUCTION, *THE WAY WE WERE*

After leaving grammar school in 1957, Bill
Ridgway worked in a succession of jobs before
gaining a teaching certificate. He later combined
a teaching career with educational writing,
producing almost 100 books over 30 years. On his
retirement from teaching, he wrote the monthly
articles included here for the Staffordshire
Evening Sentinel publication *The Way We Were*.
Bill is married with two children nad lives in the
Staffordshire Moorlands.

THE ARTWORK THROUGHOUT THIS BOOK IS BY ADAM

The photo on page 144 is courtesy of Mervyn Edwards, from the book *Potters in Parks*.

CHURNET VALLEY BOOKS
1 King Street, Leek, Staffordshire. ST13 5NW 01538 399033
thebookshopleek.co.uk
© Bill Ridgway and Churnet Valley Books 2004
ISBN 1 904546 09 9

Printed and bound by Bath Press

PREFACE

I was sufficiently encouraged by the response to the articles I wrote for *The Way We Were* to seek their publication in a book - so here it is.

I have tried to group the articles into themes to give my story structure. Consolidating a variety of articles written over six years can have the unfortunate consequence of highlighting any repetition and inconsistency, and I hope you will indulge me where this has been the case. Put it down to lapses of memory - mine, not yours.

If, through sharing my uncomplicated, but to me wonderful Post-War childhood, you enjoy fond memories of your own, my venture will have proved worthwhile.

SECTIONS

1 Schooldays   page   5

2 Wheels   page   25

3 Faces   page   47

4 Places   page   63

5 More Places   page   93

6. Work and Play   page   111

7 A Mosaic of Memories   page   137

8 Winter Tales   page   165

St Mary's, Tunstall: "pointing a sooty finger at the Lime Street skies."
Courtesy of the Warrilow Collection, Keele University Library.

SCHOOLDAYS

I look back with pleasure on my schooldays. My early years were warmly-wrapped, mysterious and kindly, a cocooned extension of home far away from the checklists, target setting and 60 second jargon of modern schooling which has debased childhood for many.

At school I felt sure, at ease and strangely free. There was no prescriptive curriculum, no propaganda, no clappy intrusions, no centralising edict, certainly no back-of-the-envelope Bright Idea. An easy control was exercised and within its gentle grasp we were let be.

I failed the 11+ but gained entry to Hanley High School, the local grammar, two years later. Advocates of the one size fits all comprehensive are fond of telling me the 11+ segregated the school population into Us and Them, and that this was immutable. I am proof it wasn't. There was flexibility up to the age of 16, and, at least in the Potteries, deserving 'late developers' were found places in the local grammars. These were often children from working class backgrounds. For some it was a passport to a world glimpsed through the nets, and then only dully.

Among my schooldays articles I have included two which refer to my time as a young teacher in the early 1960s. I hope you won't find these out of place here. As in the other pieces, I have set out to capture that zeitgeist of orderly pursuit which characterised English society at that time.

Chapters

1. A Cockney in the Schoolyard (April 1998)

2. Thrills and Spills (May 1998)

3. The Smell of Beeswax (June 1998)

4. A Bash Street Kid (Jan 1998)

5. Cruel to be Kind (Aug 2000)

6. Paying my Dues (July 2000)

7. Biros (July 2003)

8. A Sense of Order (June 2003)

1. A COCKNEY IN THE SCHOOLYARD

St Mary's Infants School, Tunstall, was situated in Lascelles Street opposite a soot-blackened Victorian brewery. The headmistress was Miss Featherstone, a dapper, bird-like woman who had witnessed every trick in the juvenile book. Our teacher was Miss Riley. She was the physical opposite - tall, buxom and motherly.

I attended St Mary's in the final year of the war. I was a London refugee, and spoke at that time in snatches of vivid Cockney which my peers took in their stride but which caused ripples of amusement among local adults.

There were daily reminders of conflict even in that far-flung outpost of city life. Behind the school stood an emergency water storage tank. Miss Riley's nature-table preambles often led to incomprehensible asides on food shortages and the prospect of victory. A palpable excitement hung in the air.

On one occasion we were asked to bring a container from home. Why? It was to be a surprise and a treat. To my mind, altruism and size were an item. The following day I came to school with the largest tin in the class. It had once contained milk powder, and must have stood at least nine inches in height.

"Isn't your tin a bit big?" Miss Riley enquired, staring hard through her thick spectacles.

"It's all we got, Miss."

"Well, you can only have the same as the others, you know."

Our treat was chocolate powder, sent to schools throughout the country by the Americans, we were told. Miss Riley ladled it with a scoop into our outstretched containers, one scoop to each. It smelled delicious, and tasted better. On dismissal the entire school went home sporting chocolate moustaches, cheeks and chins. Occasionally, nowadays, some chance-bought confectionery yields the same sweet, pervasive smell and the years roll back.

A speciality at St Mary's was a plywood mock-up of a town road, light grey for the streets, red for the houses. From a revered box, those who finished their sums first were sometimes allowed to take a die-cast assortment of cars, buses and lorries to play with. Miss Riley coached us in a one-liner should Miss Featherstone happen to come into the room.

"You're to say you're doing road safety. What do you say?"

"We're doing road safety, Miss Riley."

"That's right. You're practising road safety and don't you forget it."

At one time a spate of thieving took place in the cloakroom. Some of the children complained they had had money taken from their coat pockets. Ever vigilant, Miss Featherstone had apparently hid Clouseau-like in a recess and kept watch. Within a week the culprit was apprehended. Not because Miss Featherstone had actually seen him stealing, but betrayed by his gang, to whom he had boasted and proved his deed by displaying his purchase: a couple of new tennis balls.

Outside, a ramshackle corrugated roof spanned a length of wall adjacent to the school buildings. This was our shelter during inclement weather, the scene of fights and a storage place for the maypole.

Neither the Germans nor the British Spring could quell Miss Riley's ardour for pagan ritual. Black plimsolls were considered essential, though allowances were made for those who had only the boots they came to school in. Multi-coloured ribbons dangled from pole to shoulder, and we were prescribed one each. At a given signal a pre-rehearsed dance began, an awkward weaving in and out of bodies punctuated by the impatient trilling of Miss Riley's Acme Thunderer.

"No. Over, not under. Watch Judy do it. Now you try. One, two, three...."

The High Street newsagent's at the bottom of Lascelles Street still exists. Some lunch-breaks I would visit the shop out of bounds to purchase a Beano and breathe in the scent of printers' inks, another poignant evocation of memory.

It was while engrossed in a comic that the end of the war was announced. I did not know it was the end of the war, or what "the war" was, but it had ended. In Pinnox Street, where we lived with my father's relations, candle-lit bottles festooned the backs, fires roared and backyards disgorged neighbours bent on celebration.

My days at St Mary's were drawing to a close.

2. THRILLS AND SPILLS

I left St Mary's Infant School and went to Chell Primary. This was a gaunt, unwelcoming building which had been erected on one of those wind-swept plots beloved of the Victorians, who no doubt believed that topography and probity were somehow linked. The building was demolished a few years ago and a nursing home now occupies the site.

Boys and girls used separate entrances. Our teachers were male, the girls' female. Adjacent to the school and parallel to High Lane was a prefabricated block where Mr Toft took us for woodwork and Mr Abson for music.

A steep side street sloped to the Chatterley-Whitfield mineral line as it emerged from a short tunnel. Almost opposite the school stood a tall steam vent, incongruously sited in a bungalow garden.

Winter mornings were spent on a narrow expanse of asphalt, overlooked by a range of Dickensian classrooms. A skeetering of snow was all it took to make the first slide. As if by telepathy, a site would be selected and the process of slide creation begin. Boy after boy would hurl himself with military precision down the appointed route, the line never faltering until the ground under their steel-shod boots had been burnished to a treacherous sheen. Faster ran the skaters in the quest for thrills and glory, threadbare jersey sleeves mannequin-stiff, snot leaving glistening trails down each upper lip.

All that would stop once it was time to go inside. Out would come Polly Rubber-Neck or his sidekick, Mr Selmon, who wore a trilby and who was lame in one leg. A blast on the whistle and the heroes froze as hard as the ground. A second and lines formed.

"Stand to attention. Up straight. Ready, in lines... wait for it... Quick MARCH!"

I encountered Milly Molly Mandy and The Secret Seven under the rafters. I learned that George Stephenson couldn't read or write, and for all I knew couldn't make a slide either. Sums poured down in gills, pints and quarts and strode across the page in chains, furlongs and even leagues.

"You've got all these sums wrong, Ridgway. You divide by 12 to get pence into shillings, not 20. Twenty is shillings into pounds."

Winter turned to Spring and a new game involving the thrills and spills of the last. A boy would stand in the middle of the playground and slowly turn. Another boy would grip his waist, another his and so on for as long we could make the line. As the wheel turned the boy at the end, moving as fast as his legs could carry him, would be forced to hang on like grim death. If the line broke he was likely to be thrown against a wall. Like slide-making, this merited no disapproval from the staff and therefore must have been within the bounds of legality.

The memory can be tricked into thinking summers were always sunny and winters brought the snow. However, I cannot recall in recent years the November fogs that seemed to shroud the school in those days.

Often, making my way home for dinner or at the end of the afternoon I found myself caught up in thick, swirling tendrils through which I dared myself to hurry, listening to my own muffled footsteps and elated by the mystery of this new, secret land.

There was only High Lane to cross, and in those days you could thread a daisy chain in the middle of the road and be undisturbed for hours. On to Chell Green Avenue, the dim outlines of gables grey as the mist, grey puddles muddying my socks, and puddles and houses locked into the same cut-off world.

"Where've you been with your shoes? Look at your trousers! You're covered from head to toe."

"It was misty, Mum. I couldn't see where I was going."

"Take your trousers off. Dry 'em in front of the fire."

"What about my shoes?"

"Put 'em on the fender. You'll have to wipe 'em over before you go back."

"The elastic's gone in my garters."

"Eat your dinner."

Mr Toft taught us how to make first a boat and then a towel roller. I can't remember what happened to my wooden freighter, but the towel roller, proudly attached to our door, served its purpose for many years. From him we learned mastery over the chisel and plane, as well as ourselves.

As I write I see the glue pot bubbling like a witches' cauldron and hear the faint sounds of singing from Mr Abson's class next door.

"As sweet Polly Oliver lay musing in bed.

"A sudden strange fancy came into her head...."

And inevitably, the dull clump of his slipper as song-refusers paid their dues......

3. THE SMELL OF BEESWAX

Our estate had grown rapidly since the war and Chell Primary could no longer meet the demands placed upon it. By 1949 a new school had been erected.

Chell Heath Juniors encapsulated the mood of growing optimism then felt throughout the country. It was a symbol of hope for the future, just as the building at Chell had been an emblem of Victorian austerity.

Even as a child of nine I found the difference striking. No raftered ceilings and gothic windows here; instead a suffusion of light. Not the shafts of light begrudgingly granted from above, but a panorama of light from a profusion of windows. No more bottle-green dadoes: here the plaster was new and did not smell of mildew.

The headmaster was Mr Pipe. The fact that he smoked a pipe seemed one of those unremarkable associations one takes in one's stride when young. He had an office in the administration wing near a hall which smelled of beeswax and around which the caretaker always seemed to hover. Our teacher was Miss Martin. For me, they represented the entire school and seemed as much a buoyant product of the post war years as the building they worked in.

Our classroom overlooked an internal court. In summer, Miss Martin would open the French windows and a rosy fragrance would pervade the room as we painted at our easels. Swarms of bees would assault the berberis and cotoneaster which grew in profusion across the flags.

"A break for poetry," Miss Martin would announce, waiting for us to rinse our brushes and rest our heads as, after an introductory cough, she picked up a well-thumbed book of verse:

> *"On either side the river lie*
> *Long fields of barley and of rye,*
> *That clothe the wold and meet the sky;*
> *And thro' the field the road runs by*
> *To many tower'd Camelot;*
> *And up and down the people go,*
> *Gazing where the lilies blow*
> *Round an island there below,*
> *The island of Shalott....."*

It may have been Mr Pipe who inaugurated the tradition of Christmas concerts in the school. The festive season brought together a disparate group of cleaners, dinner ladies and pupils, although I cannot recall any member of staff being involved in the visible events.

The festooned hall would be crammed with pupils seated cross-legged on the floor, eagerly awaiting the proceedings; Mr Pipe would confer busily with Miss Martin about Things Which Did Not Concern Us, while the rallied ranks of performers took up their positions by the doors at the back of the hall.

I remember one occasion when the caretaker was called upon to sing. He did not make his way to the stage, as had other performers, but remained at the rear of the hall. In order to see him our 300 necks were obliged to make a 180-degree turn. His face had the rubicund tinge associated with a surfeit of Christmas cheer or high blood pressure. After a false start which increased his initial trepidation, he broke into a rendering of Take A Pair of Sparkling Eyes which Gilbert and Sullivan would have been hard put to recognise.

I have a picture of him in my mind's eye, his bloodshot eyes raised to the ceiling, his mouth describing a wide O as he hit the top note. The final bar of his song was greeted with a hushed and not altogether reverent silence until Mr Pipe instigated a round of applause by suddenly remembering to clap.

A medley of turns followed, culminating in someone playing the musical spoons. It may have been the caretaker - I can't remember. I do, however, remember the enthusiasm with which the final burst of applause was given, and our happy exit into the snow at dusk.

It was the end of term. In less that a week my father would carry a second-hand Raleigh up the stairs to my bedroom and my brother and I would share a pillow case bulging with fruit, the latest Rupert annual, a Meccano set, a football and posh chocolates individually wrapped. The luxurious smell of roast chicken and baked potatoes would waft from the kitchen while the world on the far side of the window lay muffled under a thickening blanket of snow.

Chell Heath Juniors marked the end of my primary school days. The time would come in the non-too-distant future when my mother would be forced to yield to my insistence on long trousers and a case to carry my books in. The trousers came in due course. But the case - who needed a case for books if he was destined for the local secondary modern?

4. A BASH STREET KID

I failed the 11-Plus in 1951 and went to Chell Secondary Modern, which in those days shared a campus with Hanley High School. A trenchant divide existed between the two, which was not entirely academic. The secondary school boys occupied a series of hastily-erected Nissen huts, whereas the high school pupils had the advantage of a spacious Post-Deco building boasting all the accoutrements of academe - laboratories, well-lit art rooms, etc, etc.

A retaining wall ran between the two institutions. Bash Street Kids to the west, High School Scholars to the east. By accident or design the local topography complemented this rift. To reach the huts one had to descend a flight of steps into Hell. To reach the high school one ascended into Heaven.

We were asked off-handedly one day if any of us wished to enter for the 13-Plus examination. I raised my hand and duly took a series of tests in which I had to describe 'An Invention Which Has Changed The World', complete such lines as 'Dance is to ballet as singing is to...' and computate the answers to problems involving the rate at which water would discharge down a drain of given dimensions.

Some weeks later I was called to the Headmaster's office. For the first time I found myself treading the Hallowed Precinct. With some trepidation I approached his door and knocked.

"Come in."

A vague smell of pipe-smoke lingered in the air. The Head stood behind an uncluttered desk, his gown displaced below one shoulder as if my knock had caught him in the act of dressing.

"Well, Ridgway, I'm pleased to tell you you've been awarded a place at the high school. Are you happy about that?"

"Yes, Sir," I mumbled.

"I expect your parents will be pleased?"

"Yes, Sir. They will."

And they were. Especially my father, although I suspect his pleasure was in part vicarious.

On September 9, 1953, in the company of perhaps six others from the council estate who had gained a place at Grammar School, I caught the free bus for the first time. It took me to Bucknall, where a new, even more prestigious Hanley High School had been built. I was overawed by its size, its entrance-cum-tower, its patioed administration wing, tiered lecture theatre, grandiose hall, grand piano and Modigliani prints. Most of all I was overawed by the staff, gowned and far from what I had considered *real life.*

My father had also been lucky. After leaving the Metropolitan Police and taking a series of dead-end jobs, he had been fortunate enough to secure a place at Training College. The serious shortage of teachers in the years immediately after the war had led the Government to introduce a one-year Emergency Training Scheme. At the age of 37, and taking PE as his main subject, he qualified as a primary school teacher.

We were now a family of five. The old Hanley High School buildings at Chell had been given over to the expanding Secondary Modern and the disintegrating Nissen huts fell into disuse. By the time my sister, who was then five, grew up, they had disappeared entirely.

In those days school and leisure were equal partners. The word 'stress' was rarely heard outside the building or engineering industries. For those who were unfortunate enough not to have lived their youth in the 1950s, clichés such as 'carefree days' and 'halcyon life' may be cynically perceived as the product of a writer's rose-tinted imagination. They are not. At least, not in my case. With cycling companions I expanded the boundaries of my world. Each summer weekend would bring a fresh perspective, a different view. With a pack of sandwiches and a shared Tizer we ventured first to Whitmore, where, before the days of the Reviled Anorak, we sat by the tracks and underlined locomotive numbers in one of Ian Allan's trainspotting books.

Ever bolder, we cycled to Manifold Valley, Dovedale, Uttoxeter and Crewe. By the age of 14 I was a seasoned explorer who, alongside the obligatory Tizer and sandwiches, had a pre-marked Ordnance Survey map, a watch to time our journeys and thus work out our average speed, and a small draw-bag of essential tools.

Thus armed we made morning forays to far-flung outposts: Oswestry, Llangollen, Manchester and Shrewsbury. And on non-cycling weekends, before the advent of 'Don't' notices, cars and regimen, we would paddle a log across Knypersley Lake, ignorant of either danger or depth, until the summer dusk hazed the Warder's Tower.

Neither play nor school were frenetic. Intertwined with homework sessions barely lasting more than an hour were visits to Smallthorne blood-tub, Bradeley Fair, and, in the company of adults 'done up in their best', to the pet-galleries at Hanley Market.

I used to think then, as I do now, that had Stoke-on-Trent retained its terraces and kilns, repaired, repainted and sandblasted, then those Victorian tentacles which held the city firmly in their grip until the 1960s would have drawn many an eager tourist, as well as helping retain the distinct character the city now lacks.

'Struggling up the incline': Edward VII leaving Whitfield Colliery.
The William Jack Collection

'Through meadowsweet scented lanes': Potteries' schoolchildren, around 1950.

5. CRUEL TO BE KIND

It was one of those bright, misty mornings in late October when the first bronze tints vied with fading green in the hedgerows. Our route was via Eaves Lane, up to Wetley Moor and back to the main road by way of Brookhouse Lane. As always, Norman Downs, our scarred games master, prescribed the rules before we set off.

"No skiving." He emphasised the order by slapping Sandy, the truncated cricket bat smoothed to a sheen through its encounter with many bottoms, against his track suit. "I want you all back here within the hour."

"But, sir -"

"No exceptions." By way of a challenge he brandished the bat aloft. "I want no skivers on this run. I know all about the backward-facing brigade. And don't bother taking any short-cuts. I know them all. I shall get to hear about it. That's a promise."

I risked a sideways glance at those who were about to achieve such Herculean feats. A motley crew had formed a half circle around Norman. Every height and weight was represented. Some were corpulent shirkers, skin the colour of cod. Others were dark, lean and nervous as whippets. Sprinkled amid the throng were greater mortals, weight-training adonii disdainful of vest and sporting cut-back shorts which contrasted starkly with the knee-length Matthews' bags worn by the rest of us.

Downs had seen it all before. Cross country got us out of his hair for an hour. It was all quite legitimate. "It's 10 o'clock, I want you back here by 11. Any questions?"

Nobody asked Norman questions. Least of all me. He flung wide the doors and gestured with Sandy towards the inviting autumnal air. "Right. Go and enjoy yourselves."

We barged out, our relief at being set free tempered only by visions of what lay in store. At first the going was good. We loped happily through the gates and along Corneville Road, chatting amicably. Some had already braved the chill by removing their shirts. We struggled across Werrington Road, in the 1950s practically devoid of traffic, and bunched once more by the pub at the far side.

A decorative corner-stone marked the start of Eaves Lane and our ascent to the moor. The tarmac now took on a harder, more threatening aspect. The line thinned, the more portly began their fight for breath as the whippets padded on. Half way up and whole columns had halted in a quest for oxygen. This was the upward grind that separated the wheat from the chaff, or from the merely overweight. A pack of Craven A was produced from somewhere. Gasp and last gasp had become synonymous in this quest for survival.

Eventually the line crested the rise, most facing the right way, but the inevitable plodder walking backwards in a futile attempt to ward off the stitch. Some unfortunates had already succombed, and could be seen crumpled to agonised hairpins by the wall.

Mindful of the time, we moved on. The narrow lane now skirted an expanse of scrub and solitary wind-bent trees amid hummocks of gorse and reedy pools. The sun had banished the mist from the heights to illuminated pockets which hid the city from view. On we plodded, oblivious to pain, puddles, muck and mud. Even the normally garrulous were forced into a pitiful silence.

The blue sky swam. We were immune to the twigs which snapped underfoot, scraped skin and faces made hideous in their quest for air. Our legs screamed for Brookhouse and the twisting descent which marked the beginning of the end of our journey.

Then we were on it, our plimsolls slap-slapping the now welcoming asphalt, no longer a foe to gravity but its bosom pal. Although the class had stretched chewing-gum thin along the route, whippers and walruses, smokers and nonsmokers, the weak, the wise, the willing and wanting were united in their thirst for rest.

The happy band which had chortled through Hanley High School's gates an hour ago returned a more subdued lot. Norman greeted us, arms crossed, a sadistic smile barely visible beneath the scar.

"Get a shower."

"I'm sorry, sir, I've forgotten to bring a a towel." He turned his pale eyes on me slowly. "I'll borrow one, sir," I mumbled

He could nod acceptance without moving his head. "You've got just five minutes. When you've finished you can all line up in the gym. It's time we did a few exercises."

6. PAYING MY DUES

"You've been playing soccer in the Third Form corridor, Ridgway."

"Yes, sir."

"And you admit to having smashed the light fitting?"

'Yes, sir. Sorry, sir."

The headmaster seemed to ponder my case, his deep-set eyes under the tufted eyebrows never leaving my face.

"It's not what I would have expected of you."

"No sir."

His stare continued to penetrate, perhaps in anticipation of further admissions of guilt or a few words in mitigation. There were none I could offer. There had been four of us kicking at a ball of paper. I had drawn the short straw. Its upward trajectory had caught the light and brought it down. I had reported it to a teacher, thinking perhaps a mild rebuke would suffice. And a bill, of course. But Dr Gardner was not to be so easily deflected. Justice not only had to be done; it had to be swift and equal in stature to the offence committed.

Abruptly he turned to a glass-fronted cupboard and twisted the swivel catch. The door swung open in eager anticipation of retribution. Canes of various sizes occupied a shelf within easy reach. He chose a particularly sinister version and flexed it appreciatively. How many? One? Two? More? How did my crime compare with the tally of petty insubordinations carried out daily at the school?

"I'm afraid I shall have to reprimand you," he went on - as if I'd not quite grasped the idea.

He levered my right hand to a convenient height and brought the cane down from above his shoulder. It caught my fingers at the second joint. There was a sudden, searing pain followed almost immediately by a sick numbness.

"Now the other."

He repeated the dose across my left hand. Now my fingertips bore the brunt. I lowered my arm. He replaced the cane, closed the glass-fronted door and turned the catch.

"You can leave now. Ask the secretary for a bill before you go back to your class."

"Yes, sir."

"No more football in the corridor?"

"No, sir."

"All right, Ridgway. Go back to your form."

I collected a bill from Brenda, our glamorous Hanley High School secretary who worked in an outer office, stuffing the chit in my blazer pocket as I left. By now a pulsating heat was coursing through my swollen fingers. The blue serge, even the slip of paper, was painful to the touch.

Knowing heads turned in the Spanish class, but nothing was said. I had paid the first instalment on my dues. I'd learnt my lesson. I wouldn't bring down any more light fittings. I took my seat and picked up my Parker. Unable to feel it, my grip was awkward and my writing suffered. But by the end of the lesson the pain had eased. I flushed with pride that I could endure such suffering and recounted the experience to a circle of admirers at break.

I was to pay two further visits to the Head's office, once for jumping from the gym roof (a doffer), and once for 'skiving off' games during a cold snap when I wasn't feeling up to it. The gym episode cost me further swollen fingers; absenteeism was considered more heinous and merited four strokes, two of which were delivered on the bottom.

I neither questioned nor resented my punishments. I didn't need a retinue of social workers and education psychologists to sort out my problems and in consequence the taxpayer was freed an extra burden. I shouldn't have engaged in horseplay. I knew it at the time and received my just deserts. The school wasn't insured for fools who might easily have injured themselves or others jumping from a roof and there's nothing like a set of stinging fingers to bring home the error of your ways. I shirked no more games; in fact, I joined the cross-country team.

Oh for the days of simplicity, of a consensus of right and wrong and no value-free transatlantic psychobabble to show us how wrong we are to condemn little Johnny for throwing his baby-sitter in the canal. Dr Gardner gave me security and helped me take responsibility for my actions. He provided a valuable service to society. I'm indebted to him. And I have no intention of pleading for recompense on the grounds that my brush with the glass-fronted cupboard made the rest of my life a tragic nightmare.

7. BIROS

For some years after I started teaching, writing in anything but ink was forbidden. Although the ball-pen (we used to call it a Biro after its inventor) had become increasingly popular in day-to-day life, schools resisted change until well into the 1960s.

However, the convenience of the ball-point pen, with its blot-free neatness and ease of use, eventually won the day. By the early 1970s most schools, if not actively welcoming this dangerous trend, at least turned a blind eye to it.

A huge cupboard which had probably occupied the same space since the turn of the century was home to the paraphernalia of the working day. Its capacious interior housed battered copies of 1930s' text books, collections of stories in the heroic tradition (*Scott of the Antarctic, Florence Nightingale*), chipped rulers, pens, pencils and ink.

The pens rose like porcupine quills from a drilled base. The stems were of wood the thickness of straw, and most contained indigo-stained nibs in various stages of disintegration. A small lozenge tin held spare nibs. When the class began writing and the inevitable complaints arose, the offending nib had to be withdrawn from the stem and replaced from the supply in the tin.

This wasn't always easy. Stubborn nibs could be difficult to remove and left a trademark stain on the fingers. Busy staff would sometimes leave this replacement activity to the pupils - with predictable results. I came to the aid of many a struggling charge who had managed to do a 'Uri Geller' on a nib which nevertheless refused to be parted from its shaft.

On the cupboard stood two further items essential to the production of 'high literature' - a dispenser, and its companion, a bottle of concentrated ink. To produce ink of an acceptable strength, at the same time avoiding clogging the nib, was a skilled job. Any classroom work involving the addition of water is a hazardous procedure and the one thing concentrated and powdered inks had in common was their ability to wreck your Raelbrook.

I usually watered down the concentrate myself after first decanting a small quantity into the dispenser. This was a funnelled can, and would hold around a litre of ink when full. It was then up to the ink monitor to fill empty inkpots - white porcelain cups which fitted into a hole in the desk top.

Blots, smudged lines and scratched characters which seemed to have been formed under torture were the consequence of using stick pens. Nibs frequently splayed or buckled under pressure (as did the staff) and inky finger prints accompanied many a text. On the whole, girls were neater than boys. On the other hand, boys were able to use their ink more creatively, producing pellets from ink-soaked blotting paper when they thought my back was turned.

I remember a sharp intake of breath when I requested ball pens for the first time around 1967. Heads of Departments had been called to a meeting in the headmaster's office. He told us there was a small amount of money remaining in the requisitions kitty. Was there an item any of us desperately wanted?

Audaciously, I said I would like to donate my stick pens to Hanley Museum and move on. Move on? Move on to what? It was then I dropped my bombshell. "I'd like a box of Biros," I said. "About a hundred - just to see how things go."

An uneasy silence followed my request. The faces of older members of staff betrayed conflicting emotions: Not writing in ink? The favoured medium of Shakespeare, Dickens and Austen? Standards would plummet. The literary canon would crumble. Pupils would resort to slipshod, careless ways. The universe would implode. On the other hand........

The head smiled condescendingly. "All right. I'll get the secretary to order a batch." He refrained from tutting: "These young teachers with their modern ways ... still, at least he's keen ... no harm to indulge him ... I was young and idealistic once...."

I got my pens. Over the next few weeks a trickle of colleagues beat a path in secret to my door. "You haven't got half a dozen Biros I could borrow, Bill? I've run out of nibs. Let you have them back at break."

Foremost in the queue were those who had tut-tutted at the meeting. But how could I refuse? I had made a heroic stand for reform. I had struck a blow for common-sense. Now we were all Enemies of The Blot.....

8. A SENSE OF ORDER

What I remember most about my early teaching career is the sense of order. Desks occupied ordered rows in each classroom. Pupils formed orderly queues en route to assembly. Lessons followed the sequential pattern prescribed by Ronald Ridout or some other text book writer, in which consecutive chapters were adhered to with military precision throughout the year. The final afternoon of term was spent in orderly pursuits, while the smell of beeswax and fresh paint heralded a super-ordered classroom on the first day back.

Likewise, punishment was meted out under an ordered code understood by staff and pupil alike. Summary justice was dispensed for rudeness, chewing in class, recalcitrant behaviour, answering the teacher back and other acts of petty insubordination. A brief warning was followed by a stroke of the cane. This had a marvellous effect, not only upon the recipient but on the rest of the class, who were thereafter mindful of their own ps and qs. Nor was the effect transient; a single stroke was usually sufficient to maintain order throughout the remainder of the term. You will recall that, as a pupil, I suffered a similar fate. It kept me good for the next 50 years.

Most ordered of all was the pupils' application to work. In many classrooms the loudest sounds were the hiss of nib on paper and an occasional whisper. Most teachers assumed an effortless authority over their charges.

My first teaching post, in 1960, was at Abbey Hulton Junior School. I remember the deputy head, Jim Wood, was a stickler for discipline. A gaunt character in Captain Mainwaring glasses and clipped moustache, Jim still maintained order from a high Victorian desk. Yet I rarely heard him - or anyone else for that matter - raise a voice in admonition.

Staff and pupils alike knew what was expected of them, and even the sinners were aware of the unwritten code they transgressed. At that time the city couldn't afford legions of experts to tell them such expectations were restrictive and damaging to the child's emotional development, so pupils were spared the neurosis of licence and grew up balanced as a result.

Assemblies occupied their own niche in this ordered scholastic day. At nine sharp, mute crocodiles were escorted to the hall to take part in Christian worship and secular dictat. The religious component taught pupils to be grateful for finding themselves under the wing of an authority zealous in its regard of their moral stature.

This theme was amplified by a strident Victorian hymn, meted out in strict tempo by a staff pianist. Depending on time or season, we ploughed the fields and scattered, were valiant against disaster, trod the verge of Jordan or watched over the Infant in a lowly cattle shed. For some reason I also recall crystal seas.

There were always some teachers less inclined to keep order than others. Those who found the going hard suffered at the hands of classes who soon learnt to exploit what they saw as a weakness. Many a merciless miscreant welcomed the diversion afforded by such lessons. In particular, I remember a music teacher whose penchant for Rossini's *William Tell* was legendary. She would lose no opportunity to play the overture in the vain hope, perhaps, that its up-beat tempo would instil order into her captivated charges where she had failed.

The result was the opposite of what she had intended. Most of the pupils gave a personal rendition of their folk hero. This usually consisted of arrow attacks on the teacher, using the piano in place of a circle of covered wagons. Some pupils, carried away on a wave of romantic nostalgia, commandeered positions outside the room and fired their imaginary arrows through the plate glass.

Notwithstanding these deviations, strict order was the rule. Indeed it was not unknown for parents to fall within its ambit. I knew of one headmaster in the early 1960s who, confronted by an irate parent, greeted him with, *"You can get that off before you come in here."*

He was referring to the man's cap, which he had kept in place en route to the head's office. I am told the parent did as he was asked, so he at least was spared a stroke of the cane.

Such incidents were rare since at the time everyone had a clear sense of what constituted order. Defining 'out of order' was therefore a far less complex (and litigious) task. Oh, for the simplicities of yesteryear.

WHEELS

The late Fifties and early Sixties marked a transition in transport. The steam locomotives whose numbers I had faithfully recorded at Crewe, Whitmore and Madeley, were shortly to be destined for the scrap-heap, as were the branch lines and innumerable mineral tracks which ran through the Potteries.

For the first time car ownership was no longer confined either to the professional classes or to those 'in trade', and my father was able to acquire a succession of vehicles prone to various degrees of trouble, a trait soon to be inherited by myself.

However, my favoured mode of transport made scant demands on my meagre resources, and throughout my teenage years we were virtually inseparable. My bike, a knocked-together affair boasting five Derailleur gears, was my escape route to regions unexplored far beyond the purlieus of Chell.

Within the space of five years my various wheels took me from the local off-licence, where I found I could jam my father's quart of mild into an antiquated saddle bag, to the Costas - then in an embryo stage of destruction.

Chapters

1. A Glorious Time to be Alive (August 1999)

2. Into the Hills (May 2000)

3. A Race Against Time (May 2001)

4. Watching Trains go by (July 1998)

5. Railway Nirvana (June 1999)

6. The Car-Van Man (Oct 2002)

7. Garden Shed Car Mechanics (Feb1998)

8. A Great Adventure(Jan 2002)

'Chapped hands and heatless fires': snowy scenes in the Moorlands .

'A garden front and back': Council houses being built in Stoke after the Second World War.

1. A GLORIOUS TIME TO BE ALIVE

In many ways, the Victorian zeitgeist cast its shadow over the 1950s. Modern Times were invented in 1962, along with The Beatles.

Each facet of Potteries' life in the decade following the war was rooted in a previous generation's experiences. Drays were still to be seen, hauled by plodding shires; long-buried tram lines were laid bare by excavators' picks; umbilical entries continued to link adjacent streets; terraces built a hundred years earlier formed the bulk of the housing stock and identified both the locality and those who lived in it. The ubiquitous bottle-oven still added its smoke to the general pall.

Things were about to change, but during that brief interlude I had a glimpse of Potteries' life as it must have been before I was born, before my grandfather was born. The skyline had altered little since the 1930s, when those postcards depicting a scarred industrial landscape and a satirical "When Stoke smokes..." were circulated - a scene little changed from a century before.

But it was not only the city that lay frozen under a permafrost of time. The countryside, too, harboured a pre-car tranquility the present-day motorist would be hard put to recognise. There was a growing population of car-users, but they formed a minority. And those fortunate enough to own a Hillman Minx seemed to use if for nothing more adventurous than the work run, with an occasional weekend foray to Aunty Ethel's in Penkhull. So the countryside was left to intrepid cyclists like myself, who with a pack of sandwiches and a bottle of mineral water made far-flung excursions into the unknown.

There was no housing sprawl then. Biking from Chell to the Peak, the once magnificent and now ruined valley which runs through Baddeley Green was a gateway to freedom and a thousand miles from the City boundary. Passing cars were infrequent enough to be noted, the air was breathable and foreign parts consisted of the sporadic villages which lay en route.

Inevitably, our destination was Dovedale. In the height of summer it rang with bird song, the river murmured between the stepping stones and cars and car parks had yet to put in an appearance. The valley attracted only a sprinkling of visitors, back packers and cyclists like ourselves who had made the weekend trip over the hills from Sheffield, Derby, Nottingham and Stoke. Sometimes we would travel west. To Chester through meadowsweet-scented lanes or to the Welsh foothills, which we could reach in less than three hours against a stiff breeze. I was as fit as a butcher's dog, as were many of my generation. Not a fitness packaged in lycra and gyrating to muzak, but a rude health born of pumping the pedals, unadulterated food and clean air.

Our bikes, like ourselves, were nothing to write home about. I had an antiquated Carlton racer with odd wheels. Our attire complemented this rough and ready theme: flannels and open shirt in cool weather, knee-length shorts and top in the heat. Or no top during uphill stretches in sweltering sun.

It was a glorious time to be alive. The hedgerows sparkled with flowers, and long tracts yielded no sound more grating than the distant stutter of a tractor. I had an unwavering sense of my identity then. I knew what it was to be English. I knew it not only from the smoke-blackened terraces I had left behind, but from corncockle and celandine, bluebell and grit-stone, brook and furrow. The country, the towering cumulus, the landscape and the click of my mileometer along the lanes blended like the Sunday bells cascading across Tunstall roofs from St Mary's steeple.

And as I write I hear the choir singing with gusto the old W C Dix hymn to the countryside that I explored on my ramshackle bike 50 years ago:

> *Bright robes of gold the fields adorn,*
> *The hills with joy are ringing.*
> *The valleys stand so thick with corn*
> *That even they are singing.*

The countryside around Stoke-on-Trent still exists. But not as much of it. And you have to travel further to get there. The construction industry has seen to that. I believe it's called progress.

'A glorious time to be alive!'

2. INTO THE HILLS

I never sought hills to climb on the ramshackle bikes I owned in the Fifties, but occasionally, when I felt the urge to travel east, there was no alternative. Standing in the front garden of our house looking towards Whitfield Colliery, the Morridge Moorlands rose in a whale-back behind the stack. Across intervening valleys lay villages and countryside worthy of exploration. But to reach them one had to rely on strong thighs and Derailleur gears.

A friend and I spent hours in an analysis of gear ratios derived from obscure charts. Before a run we would substitute an existing block for one more suited to the job in hand. Thus equipped, we would head for Rudyard, Leek, Dovedale, Buxton, Waterhouses or Ashbourne. Once, we reached the outskirts of Derby - foreign parts indeed.

Yet we didn't have to go as far as that to find ourselves in unfamiliar territory. Once we had cleared Brindley Ford and begun the climb towards Biddulph we were entering exotic lands. Our excitement grew as we reached Knypersley, a place of towering beeches and mock tudor semis, a far cry from our estate.

To reach Rudyard, Knypersley was a necessary stepping stone and a useful place to quench one's thirst. One then had to endure a rigorous ascent to the moors. Heads down, we developed the psychological trick of never looking further than the front wheel. That way we could convince ourselves the hill didn't really exist until we had crested the rise.

In the Fifties, work was in progress creating the Biddulph miners' estate. Enormous caterpillars trundled across the valley and uprooted hedges flared along the edge of the site. But soon the din of machinery was replaced by a constant fluting of larks which accompanied us all the way to Moortop.

The view across what is now the Staffordshire Moorlands from Top Road has changed little since my cycling days. It was, and is, a quintessential English landscape. From the heights, a glorious tapestry of fields shimmered beneath billowing cumulus. Tracts of woodland followed the slopes, their dense under-tree greens a stark counterpoint to the pastel greens of cut and uncut meadows. The land rose in steep, hazy sweeps to Roche Grange and The Roaches, and far below us a diamond ribbon slashed the valley floor - Rudyard Lake.

Electricity pylons now straddle the lane we took to Rudyard. The lines they carry could be buried for price of a director's lunch. Perhaps the notion of beauty is irrelevant to some, or worse, associated with an elitism which needs to be cured. Whatever the reason, one can edit these intrusions from the landscape and return it to its former state.

Rudyard was timelocked even then. What became The Poacher's Tavern was then the Railway Inn. It seemed discarded in the Fifties, echoing with the sighs of pre-war ghosts, its wicker chairs set for diners who never turned up and faded pictures of The Knotty hanging from faded walls.

The station it served was a couple of minutes away. I remember the tankers, with their complement of three or four coaches, hissing steam before setting off down the line to Leek. Few passengers alighted. Rudyard after the war had lost its customers to Blackpool and North Wales. And Dr Beeching saw to it that even the few who used the line would now need to buy a car.

Swallows and Amazons came in smaller numbers and spent the Wakes in 1930s cabins hidden among the lakeside trees. The shacks are still there, some dilapidated as I remember them, others made resplendant with the fresh paint and laid-out gardens one associates with a permanent dwelling. Despite the intervening years, the Thirties still clings to the fabric of the place. It is not hard to see, in the mind's eye, golfers in plus fours, their wives in cloche hats, their children scooping minnows from the shallows.

The Lake Hotel was where we turned back. Sometimes, when we were particularly well off and had the price of a Mars, we would call at a timbered lakeside cafe before the homeward journey. And if we no longer desired the challenge of the hills we would return along Dunwood Lane to join the Leek Road. This was the longer way, but easier on the muscles.

My bike has long been scrapped. The line which used to serve the village is a pleasant greenway and a favourite haunt of anglers. To cock a snook at Dr Beeching, perhaps, a miniature railway now occupies part of the old trackbed. And that wonderful pre-war ambience unaccountably persists.

3. A RACE AGAINST TIME

From time to time my old bike would be out of action and I took the bus. The fare from Chell to Tunstall was one (old) penny. There were two routes: one via Greenbank Road, the other by way of St Michael's Road and Pitt's Hill. The buses which travelled these routes were all single-deckers. Brown's used Greenbank Road and Wells' made the journey up St Michael's Road and down to Fegg Hayes via Chell roundabout.

As a child I preferred to travel up Greenbank Road for a variety of reasons, not least the bus itself. This was a slat-seated Bedford driven by a man universally known as Arthur and supervised by a thin-faced conductor who took the welfare of his passengers very seriously.

"Hang on Arthur - there's room for one at the back." Arthur would gaze resignedly ahead until the shopping-laden fare took her seat.

"All right now, Arthur." Arthur would set off. "Weigh on, Arthur, weigh on! Her's caught the wrong bus."

Passengers would titter, Arthur would resume his gaze, the conductor would begin a brisk punching of tickets, the new arrival would shuffle without embarrassment back to the door.

The prized seat was at the front alongside Arthur. My brother and I could take note of his driving skills, check the speedometer, keep our eyes on the jutting bonnet and agonise whether the vehicle was robust enough to make it up the steep Greenbank gradient without sliding out of control all the way back to Tunstall Park. I always breathed a sigh of relief when we reached the top and turned into the level security of High Lane.

Arthur was inscrutable and had no nerves. He and his conscientious conductor were an item, their attachment to their circuit as predictable as the timetable which governed their lives. No less predictable was the Wells' flyer. Where Arthur's Bedford was a less than alluring shade of brown, Wells' boasted a fleet of green buses renowned as much for their antiquity as their punctuality. The design was different, the driver compartmentalised from the passengers, the seats upholstered and rarely empty during their hourly trips to Chell.

I remember an outstanding example of such a journey, not only because on this occasion it was standing room only, but because the speed at which the vehicle was driven forced me to the conclusion the driver had taken leave of his senses.

The journey began calmly enough. A long line of home-bound workers were waiting for the bus, which arrived five minutes late. They filed on until every seat was taken and the gangway almost impassable. No sooner was the door shut than the driver, mindful of the need to make up time, was off.

In Station Road (now the Boulevard) we kept to a modest speed. Once we had made the turning into Victoria Park Road, however, our unassuming Dr Jekyll changed abruptly into Mr Hyde. I was unaware of the vehicle's increasing speed until the standing passengers began to sway. This motion intensified throughout the bus until the seated passengers too were caught in a series of violent lurching movements and began to swear, not necessarily under their breath.

Meanwhile, the large Victorian houses on the nearside were flashing by at a speed never previously experienced on that stretch of road by a Public Service Vehicle. By the time we passed the lower park gates a number of passengers could be seen fumbling for their Park Drives, and it was only the advent of St Michael's Road, with its steep upward incline, that brought the driver out of his trance. We all breathed a sigh of relief as the first passengers alighted near the Turnhurst pub.

I remember one woman in particular took it upon herself to list a verbal assessment of our man's shortcomings and made her way to the front of the bus to give him an analysis in words everyone could hear and understand.

"You're not fit to drive a ---- pram."

"I have to keep to me timetable, duck."

"Timetable, my ---. You're a madman."

"This wunna do more than 30 flat out, woman."

I don't know whether she got around to reporting him. It may have been coincidence, but after that episode the queue for Arthur's Bedford seemed to grow suddenly longer....

4. WATCHING THE TRAINS GO BY

Wells' buses ran close to the mineral line which skirted the waste land next to our estate. The land had been spoiled by now-discontinued mining. In 1946, when we moved to our new council house, many of the visible scars of industrial activity were in evidence and were to remain so for the better part of four decades.

It is difficult for those born after the Sixties to appreciate the freedom a child as young as six enjoyed in the years after the war. The marker was tea time, and as long as we appeared before five o'clock no one worried where we were or what we were doing. A sense of safety prevailed. Murders were rare enough to make headline news, the word 'mugging' hadn't been invented, and those adages beloved of the Victorians still held sway: 'cleanliness was next to Godliness', we 'ate like Christians', and 'taking something to which you were not entitled' constituted the breaking of a Commandment.

My particular freedom entitled me to seek skylarks' eggs in the wastes of tufted grass, to ride my bike through the remains of derelict mounds and to test the strength of what appeared to be a capped pit shaft by jumping into an intriguing hollow not more than a couple of hundred yards from home. However, my greatest source of innocent pleasure was watching the coal trains go by.

There were several vantage points. My favourite was a rickety footbridge which spanned a cutting a small distance from Chell Tunnel. I would cross the bridge to mid-point and await the next rumble. Sometimes a single engine would pull an entire clanking line of wagons. Occasionally the train was heavy enough to necessitate two engines, one at either end.

From the bridge, the line stretched east to Chatterley Whitfield Colliery. A distant hoot signalled an imminent departure. Within minutes the train would struggle doggedly up the incline towards my footbridge, billowing steam and emitting a cacophony of hisses and wails.

Which engine would it be this time? Minnie or Roger, Polly or Katie, Alexandra, Edward or Phoenix? I knew their names by heart. Minnie was a favourite. She would lumber defiantly between the deep clefts of shale, throwing off thick tendrils of steam which enveloped me and the bridge in vaporous smuts before plunging into the mouth of the tunnel. I would wait a further minute until the engine passed under the steam vent opposite Chell School. A white fountain would issue for a moment from the turret of soot-stained masonry. The clanking faded and died, then returned faintly as the train left the tunnel and continued its journey behind Tunstall Park.

When the mood took me I discarded the footbridge in favour of Little Chell Lane, where the line crossed the road. Here the engine would halt while the driver got out to make sure the way was clear before proceeding. Between Tunstall Park and what was to be Mill Hill estate was a vast acreage of sidings. The trains negotiated these before disappearing out of bounds in the direction of Brownhills and Longport.

The line came to an end with the demise of the colliery. The route is now a greenway for much of its length, and one which I occasionally walk - but never without a thought for the ghosts of Minnie, Roger and the rest, trundling resolutely over invisible metals to Longport.

***

My memories of the Loop Line are equally fond. From my bedroom, as a child, I could hear through the open window the comforting puff-puff of summer tankers setting out from Pittshill station with their complement of three or four coaches. From there, the line headed north west to culminate in Kidsgrove via a series of cuttings. A mile in the opposite direction was Tunstall station. Situated at the end of what is now The Boulevard, the station epitomised the sort of building one associates with branch lines built in the second half of the 19th century. Painted Victorian posters advertising day trips to North Wales and harmoniums were still visible along the station approach, and the faint odour of creosote hung in the air.

Even now I cannot visit a railway station without a feeling of exhilaration. As a child in the Forties, turning from the road into the descending path that led to the ticket office signalled a departure to exotic destinations. It seemed to me that the station and its precincts occupied a space outside the normal scurrying of life.

By the time I was 10, my inauguration into local train lore was complete. I have held a fascination for railways ever since.

5. RAILWAY NIRVANA

Yes, I admit it. I was a trainspotter. And, no, anoraks were not obligatory at that time. On the other hand, duffle coats were, and I must have acquired one from somewhere because I distinctly remember wearing it under the gantry at Crewe Station while I hung on for a 'semi', whose number I might not have in the teeth of a gale I had not bargained for.

A 'semi' was the trainspotter's prize, a huge Coronation Class locomotive fronting the Glasgow to London express. Its presence produced whoops of delight among the equally duffled sodality who had made the trip to Crewe in the hope of just such an occasion. Once streamlined but now reduced to a minimalist assemblage of valves and hisses, the growling giant came to rest at the south end of the station with a howling mass of pencil-clutchers sprinting alongside.

If you were lucky you could 'cab' it. That meant being invited to share the footplate by the driver for a few minutes before the train's departure. On rare occasions you got to eat your trainspotter's apple perched on a plank by the firebox door.

I am not sure which of the Rules for Running a Railway were infringed during this innocent pastime. Probably a whole raft of them. Certainly enough to make Dr Beeching, the hatchet-man hired by the Government to "fix" the network (at the behest of the oil companies), turn in his grave.

This kind of colonisation was common at Crewe in the 1950s. Particularly popular were sunny Saturdays in summer, when the bona fide passengers awaiting their connection were outnumbered and frequently outmanoeuvered by hordes of gibbering rail buffs clutching their Ian Allan's in anticipation of a rarity whose number could be gloated over for weeks to come. They appeared to the chagrin of passengers and staff alike, and in the most unlikely places.

Trainspotting folklore has it that one fanatic was found encamped in a disused passageway beneath Platform One. None of the staff knew how he had got there. Even the Station Master was unaware that this retreat existed. They eventually found him, perched on a makeshift seat and peering through a hole in the brickwork at track level. He was underlining the number of an antiquated shunter by the aid of a flickering torch. He now had visual contact with every locomotive in its class.

Notwithstanding the fact that his subterranean nirvana now echoed to the calls of police, railway staff and stretcher-bearers, he emerged in that state of bliss which could only be fully appreciated by true track cognoscenti. After all, he had forked out his penny and bought his platform ticket. This entitled him to regard the entire complex in the same way he might his own fireside. What was all the fuss about?

We used to catch the Crewe train at Longport, trying each time we made the journey to work out how to prove from the wheel-clicks that Harecastle Tunnel really *was* a mile long. But we never got to grips with the maths. And when money for the ticket was hard to come by, we settled for a trainspotting session at Longport itself. Unfortunately, the Staffordshire Loop was not in the same league as Crewe. It lacked gravitas. You got no buzz from watching a tanker with a load of empties plodding to Stoke and resorted to diversions instead. Ian Allan's books lay discarded in the grass in favour of a swapped Beano and sherbet dip.

Whitmore vied with Crewe for our attention. A friend and I packed our third-hand Carlton racers with cheese sandwiches and set off mid-morning to get there by lunch. Where Crewe was proud, Whitmore was pacy. Crewe brought even the mighty Devonian to a halt. At Whitmore it flew past at 80mph, sending vibrations down the track all the way to Madeley Troughs. This was the glorious stretch where one of our streamlined semis had clocked up an unheard of 114mph in the 1930s and almost come to grief on the points outside Crewe. It was a place of rabbit-burrowed sandhills and creosote, of discarded churns and lappet moths, of a time strangely suspended between past and present. The peace was the same: only the locomotives had changed, and not much.

Lulls were rare. Lines were known as Fast Up, Fast Down, Slow Up and Slow Down and having this indispensable jargon to hand was tantamount to life membership of the Wheel-tappers' and Shunters' Club. Slow trains were greeted with disdain; the ethereal palpitations which heralded a fast express sent us reaching for our pencils.

Whitmore was the place to see trains passing in multiples. The law which gave rise to this phenomenon in that location escaped me. There was definitely something spooky about it. Calculations with which I am still unfamiliar might have explained it, but these multi-train episodes seemed to me to owe as much to some unknowable formula as they did to statistical logic. On one memorable occasion I beheld four trains moving simultaneously through the cutting at varying speeds, a once-in-the-century happening, perhaps, and one which it fell on me to recount in many a scoffer's ear.

Mineral line and branch line, siding and station, goods yard and wagon shed, terminus and mallowed halt, my early years seemed to have been inextricably linked with the heat and scent of summers, just watching the trains go by.

A Great Adventure. Me on the bonnet, John Baddeley
standing - en route to Spain in 1960.

Hanley in 1953.

6. THE CAR-VAN MAN

My father's introduction to vans began with his first vehicle, an Austin 10, in 1958. Strictly speaking, the Austin was not a van, since someone had once cut windows in the sides. However, it retained a sufficiently van-ish nature to give him ideas for future purchases.

It became a noted feature of our almost car-free estate. Despite its cocking a snook at his efforts to preserve it, breaking down at regular intervals and shedding odd bits of rusty steel over the cul-de-sac where it was parked, he was inordinately proud of his car-van.

He didn't go so far as to clean it, but he was an avid servicer and repairer. He needed to be. It spent more of its life in a garage near the school where he worked than outside our house. He always drove at a steady 30, yet the Austin regarded this as a sign of weakness and made sure his wallet never strayed far from Red Alert. Even so, it was not all bad news. In fact, I learnt my rudimentary driving skills in the Austin. And when the time came for my test, I passed at the second attempt.

My father had a well-honed ritual to coax the vehicle into starting in the mornings. First he would turn the engine six times using the winding handle located in the boot (it had to be six times). The next step was to switch on the ignition and give a further three turns with the winder (it had to be three). The winding handle was then disconnected and replaced optimistically in the boot. The acid test was now upon us. The choke was pulled fully out, followed by the starter button also after a count of three (or was it four?). Fingers were crossed.

If all went well and the morning was fine and dry, the Austin would reward him by spluttering into life at the second attempt. However, should the barometer promise the merest hint of damp, he was in trouble. The only recourse then was to clutch-start the engine. Fortunately he had chosen to live on a hill with just such an eventuality in mind.

The Austin car-van occasionally provided trouble-free motoring for hours on end. Indeed, at one time two full weeks elapsed before it succumbed to the attentions of a new mechanic, this time at a roadside garage near Taunton. I had been permitted to borrow the car for a holiday in Cornwall. Given its reliability rating some might have considered this a foolhardy move on my part. And so it turned out.

Half way home I came to a halt - luckily outside the aforementioned garage. A blocked carburettor jet was diagnosed and quickly blown free and the rest of the journey passed without further incident.

Sometimes, during trouble-free periods, my father would reward his acquisition with embrocations purchased from a car accessory shop situated near the Market Square in Hanley. I particularly recall a nostrum guaranteed to improve performance amazingly. First, the spark-plugs had to be removed (this, incidentally being the summit of my father's mechanical ambitions) and a measured dose of the liquid poured down each hole. Once the job had been completed and the plugs replaced, he started the car. Dense clouds of white smoke erupted immediately from the treated engine, through which my father's silhouette danced wrathfully. He was, I thought, indicating his reluctance to accept the manufacturer's claims of optimum performance.

A friend of mine eventually offered £10 for the car-van as long as my father could guarantee its viability on the date of purchase. As it happened, the Austin was on its best behaviour and the transaction was duly completed. However, the jinx had only taken a few days off and not retired. The following week the Austin reverted to its old ways and for some unaccountable reason it began to kangaroo through the cul-de-sac, snapping the two front springs simultaneously.

An ignominious end at the scrappers now awaited it. By way of consolation, the Austin wouldn't be the last of my father's cars to make the trip. And fortunately it wouldn't be long before I had a vehicle of my own.

7. GARDEN SHED CAR MECHANICS

The Sixties are often looked upon as an era of dramatic change. Looking back, it seems the city was preparing to shed the vestiges of its Victorian past and set its sights on the coming decades.

Lime Street, Tunstall, where I spent my early years, was bulldozed into oblivion along with its entries, corner shops, vicarage and church, its provincial respectability and its borrow-a-cup-of-sugar communality. The Loop Line was prized up, the station demolished and the eponymous Station Road rechristened The Boulevard, though it was neither broad nor tree-lined. It was no accident that Dr Beeching, the huge expansion of satellite towns and the growth in car ownership happened simultaneously: orchestration isn't solely the province of music.

You are a child of your era and to a greater or lesser extent you must go with the flow. I was as eager as the rest to acquire a 'catching' set of wheels. I was 20 and had just earned my first regular wage packet. I couldn't wait to give some of my hard-earned cash to the first person who would sell me a decent car. But I didn't want any car; I wanted a car with cachet, something to turn heads. After all, I was a grown man now. I had substituted my crepes, luminous socks and drainpipes for a cravat and cavalry twills. I wasn't interested in a Hillman Hunter or a Ford Anglia. I wanted a sports car.

I lit upon an MG TA in bright red. The vendor explained to me that in some previous incarnation the original MG engine had been replaced by a Morris unit and someone had contrived a linkage between this Morris powerhouse and the MG prop-shaft in his garden shed. I was as blind to his honesty as to the timpanist under the bonnet during our test drive, and the way the doors, such as they were, dropped a full two inches on opening. Such was my delight in obtaining my own sporty transport, I paid him his thirty pounds and drove away.

Adventurously, the following month I decided to pay a surprise visit to a girlfriend who lived in north London. By some miracle the car survived the return journey as far as the entrance to Trentham Gardens, when I sensed a slight trembling under my feet. As I continued along the A34 the trembling grew to a serious vibration. I slowed the car to 10 miles an hour and plodded on.

As I approached home the entire vehicle began to lurch, the movement punctuated by a repertoire of disconcerting noises from the chassis. I had just gained the cul-de-sac opposite our house when a heavy metallic clunk sounded beneath the car. I got out and peered underneath. The entire propshaft was lying on the road. I have harboured a strong suspicion of garden-shed mechanics ever since.

The MG did not last long, and my father was kind enough to let me use his Morris Cowley van while I looked for a replacement vehicle whose strong point this time, I decided, should be dependability rather than elan.

It is something of a family mystery why my father acquired this 10 hundredweight van. As far as we knew, he was not engaged in any nefarious activity and neither did he want to keep chickens. Moreover, the passenger seat had a habit of disengaging itself from its mounting when negotiating any but the most gradual curve. This short-coming was never mentioned by my girlfriend at that time, an attractive, dark haired student from a good family who had been used to better things.

Eventually, I acquired a car that was, for a time, fairly dependable but far too big to make sense. It would be my guide through journeys to work, the world of jazz and the days that led to my marriage. Known as a Wolseley 6/80, this capacious ex-police vehicle would come to know the still nearly empty highways of three counties before it succumbed to economics and Mr McGuiness's scrapyard.

I met my future wife on our first day at the new school where we had both been allocated teaching posts. But saving up to get married meant economies and the big Wolseley hovered around the 12 miles per gallon mark. It had to go. In its place I bought an A35 van. Why a van? Better ask my father.

8. A GREAT ADVENTURE

I went abroad for the first time in 1960. I had no car at the time and my father lent me his Morris van for the fortnight. I travelled with two companions, John Baddeley and Derek Rogers. We enjoyed none of the appurtenances holidaymakers consider essential nowadays. We had the clothes we stood up in, shorts and spare underwear, a leaky spirit stove and an army blanket which had seen better days.

Our plan was to travel south as far as Barcelona and return through France by a different route. To save money, the van would double up as our dormitory, kitchen and cafe. It was to be a great adventure.

Unfortunately, things didn't go according to plan. En route to the coast, we lost our way in London (twice) and collided with another vehicle in a narrow street. Luckily the damage to the van was slight, and the driver of the other car seemed to regard the incident as just another thread in the fabric of his life. We exchanged addresses and, confident in the knowledge I would be in touch on my return from Spain, he gave me detailed instructions on how to reach Dover.

We caught an early morning ferry. As we watched Calais creep towards us in the haze, Stoke seemed a million miles away. No-one had ever made this glorious trek before. Not in a Morris van at any rate. We were Primus stove pioneers. Our quest for excitement was boundless. We would take Europe by storm.

The exhaust pipe began to blow in central France and by the time we reached Limoges the Morris had reverted to an earlier karma. Now it was roaring like a tractor. We were getting stares. We were far from Chell and being glared at. We began to feel less intrepid.

It was Derek who suggested the procedure usually adopted by those of limited means. This involved jubilee clips and a can. The idea was to cut open the can and secure it to the leaking exhaust pipe with the clips. We bought clips, a tin-opener and a couple of tins of beans and put his idea to the test. Not only did it work, but we enjoyed the haricots to boot.

We parked the van for the night in a forest glade and the next morning set off early on the last section of our downward journey. By mid afternoon we had our first glimpse of the Pyrenees on the southern horizon. From 50 miles away their peaks seemed insubstantial beneath the cloudless sky, but we soon discovered they were real enough.

My father's van was well suited to the task of ferrying him to Chell Workingmen's Club. Negotiating endless hair-pins in the gathering gloom was another matter. The crony who had sold him the van had once informed him that the Morris's column-mounted gear lever had 32 parts as opposed to the usual four. If there was a patron saint of gearsticks, now was the time to invoke his assistance.

At that time, the villagers in the passes were unused to travellers in strange vans. They were a wonderfully warm-hearted people, and nodded to us as we went by. I have a fond memory of a file of schoolboys being led by a priest to a hillside chapel. They waved as if we were passing royalty, their still-raised arms fading into the gloom of the valley as night came on.

We arrived in Barcelona exhausted. After a day's rest we began to thread our way back through the now familiar Costa Brava resorts - Calella, Blanes, Lloret de Mar. Some were little more than fishing villages with the odd hotel rising incongruously above a row of cottage roofs. Some had open sewers. Occasionally we would spot an alfresco trestle, roughly canopied and scant of custom.

Every couple of hundred miles, the wrap-around bean can suffered the same fate as the silencer but, by now, we were more canny and kept spares. Just outside Port Bou we met two students perched atop a BSA Bantam whose tyres had given up under their combined weight. It turned out they had made the journey from Market Drayton.

During the course of the ensuing conversation, one of them mentioned what was then a new arrival on the market - a cream which tanned without the sun. The Mediterranean heat had suited neither of my companions, who had spent most of the holiday under wraps. Even so, they balked at the ignominy of getting back to Chell unbronzed. We pooled what was left of our money and purchased the necessary tube. Unfortunately the instructions were in French, and after several liberal applications we awoke to find our faces had turned beetroot red.

We got back in one piece and the van spent several more summers parked outside my father's club before he sold it on. By then its moment of glory had long since passed. Ever a glutton for punishment, I plied the same route south five years later. This time I took my A35 van.

FACES

Some faces linger in the mind. Others pass by. Why I chose to write about the three members of my family included here and not others, I am not sure. There might be something Freudian in it. The one thing they have in common is that they are all deceased - as is Dr Halpin.

I remember the doctor and others who were neither friend nor family plying their trades, as people did in the Post-War years, with humour and resilience. In the main they were kind, rather than caring. An altogether different concept.

Looking at them afresh, what springs to mind is their eccentric individuality. The dull plod of conformity would not to be heard for some decades. My father cut the lawn with hedging shears, Great Uncle George cracked his leather belt for no apparent reason and Buy a Colley spent his days swiping at urchins who had designs on his livelihood.

Chapters

1. The Old Man (March 2000)

2. Great Uncle George (Feb 2000)

3. An Intrepid Voyager (Oct 2001)

4. Health to the People (Oct 1999)

5. Traps, Churns & an Alvis Pick-up (June 2001)

6. Musical Spoons (Feb 2001)

1. THE OLD MAN

My father was out of step with his times. The terraces where he grew up were more real to him than the post-war estate which now became our home, and the years between his Tunstall childhood and the time we left were never free, in his mind, of the Victorian ethos which preceded them.

His armchair was sacrosanct and reserved solely for his own use. It occupied a niche by the hearth. Close at hand were other familiar securities: a grief-stricken dictionary, a thumbed Sentinel folded at the crossword page and at least one uncapped pen. The low table which held these relics also bore occasional scraps and jottings, written when he was in the mood about his early life in Lime Street.

He remembered an uncle home from the trenches struggling with the buckles of his puttees, his mother (my grandmother) struggling with her stays and a cousin struggling with a clay-laden barrow through the mire at Platt's Brickyard. My father documented a haphazard wealth of struggles and left his memories to the mercy of tea cup rings and posterity as he himself struggled to the end.

It was always tempting to colonise my father's chair when he was out. Not because it was particularly comfortable, nor for the access it granted to the sacred corner. It was teenage rebellion that forced the issue, a tongue in cheek rebellion which could be guaranteed to produce the anticipated response when he returned home.

This could take the form of a direct order to vacate the chair. More often, however, he would stare at the illicit occupant then at the seat as a dog eyes lead and door alternately. A refusal would be intolerable, tantamount to a denial of the natural order of things. No sitter was able to bear his scrutiny for long and would slink after a face-saving interval to a corner of the room.

My father was fond of polemic and liked nothing better than to extol the virtues of the Labour Party, decry the hypocrisy of the Church and denounce the cupidity of bosses everywhere. His arguments were inconclusive, but allowed him to let off steam and gave us opportunity of disagreeing with almost everything he said. His beliefs were rooted in his class and his Potteries upbringing, and to the end he was able to separate the guys in white hats from those in black.

His ventures into DIY were eccentric, to say the least. Throughout my childhood his favoured means of repair was tape. He used this with often spectacular results on jobs as varied as ceiling cracks, torn upholstery and electrical appliances. He set great store by the adhesive qualities of his tapes, and a multicoloured selection was always available from the kitchen drawer. Each spool was part of a hierarchy of instant fixes. Strong, white tape for the cracks around ceiling flxtures, narrow, grey tape for the arms of the couch, red or green for general repairs. If tapemanship failed, as it sometimes did, a large jar of Special Glue was on stand-by.

No one but my father knew the origins of this jar, nor were we sure what it really contained. The khaki mixture stank of rotting cabbage and was so sticky we often resorted to a plumber's wrench to segregate cap from bottle. It was of the consistency of frozen butter, and had to be prized out with any sharp instrument that came to hand. Yet despite its apparent virility the glue only worked in the short term. Within a couple of weeks his dictionary, for example, had regained its former status and lay devoid of its cover amid a detritus of escaped pages.

Where both tape and glue proved inadequate, tools were called for. It will by now be apparent that my father's relationship to tools was that of a dog to Panorama: it has a vague notion that there's something it should know about, but can't quite get a handle on it.

His tools were turn-of-the-century hand-me downs. Bodged, bent and buckled, they resided in an immaculately kept box in the boot of his van. The thought of having to use them disturbed him, and to blot them out he hid them under a dark velvet cloth. Collectively worth less than a shilling, he flatly refused to replace them with something new. The hammer head was only partially attached to its stale and the jaws of his pincers hadn't met in decades. Pride of place was given to a blunt screwdriver whose handle had been charred to a shapeless mass in some long forgotten fire. Its past duties had included chisel work, paint-stirring and presumably, poker, yet he refused to compromise the set by letting it go.

It was a privilege to watch my father going about his household tasks. Shortly after the war when we moved to our estate, he set about digging a garden patch. He had come by a small edging spade which, like the screwdriver, had a partly carbonised handle. It was almost impossible to grip, and the twisted blade made digging a particularly hazardous undertaking. Yet he somehow achieved it. We mauled clods from the backs and a lawn of sorts was laid. Some weeks later, my father set about the first cut with a pair of rusty hedging shears. It took him most of the morning to complete the job.

In this age of pre-packaged identities, where the eccentricities which coloured people's lives are no longer acceptable, I find it refreshing to think back to those early years and to savour again the glorious non-conformity of an era long since gone.

I don't know whether they've got around to using Black and Decker in the celestial workshops. If they have, one thing's for certain: my father will have no truck with anything with a cord or battery attached. Not on your life. If his screwdriver was good enough in this life, it will be more than adequate in the next.

'This wunna do more than 30 flat out.' Colliery bus at Whitfield.

2. GREAT UNCLE GEORGE

My father rarely mentioned Great Uncle George. George and his sister Annie shared a Lime Street house a stone's throw from St Mary's Vicarage and opposite my grandmother's terrace. He was grandfather's brother, and partially-sighted; the result, it was said, of an accident sustained while chopping wood for the fire.

George lived a spartan life. His table stood undraped in a corner of the living room. The joints had worked loose in the three chairs which must at one time have comprised part of a set. His parlour was sparsely furnished and bare of the paraphernalia of vases and chinaware even his lowliest neighbours could boast. His one civility was a foxed print depicting an angel hovering protectively behind a child playing on the parapet of a bridge. Its frame was treacled with ancient varnish, and a mawkish Victorian caption complemented the theme. I can't remember the exact words, but they were something to the effect that God Is Our Saviour and Our Balm.

Apart from a single threadbare mat, both living room and parlour were dull with dun quarries and walls the colour of nicotine. George was a tall, stooped man and getting on for 80 as I remember him. He must have been powerful, and according to my father he returned from the Trenches a committed socialist with a decoration he had picked up in Flanders' Fields and a belt whose tongue had flapped open at the waist since the cessation of hostilities. His party-piece was to remove the belt, form a loop and snap the thick, crazed leather to produce a loud retort. He was also partial to Tizer. A bottle always had a niche in a corner of the window overlooking a blue-brick yard which neither my brother nor I were allowed to enter. The bricks, subsided in places, chipped in others, were home to lichenous growths and a rusty mangle.

By the late 1950s, George had been a widower for many years. When his sister was also widowed, she came to keep house for him. Annie seemed even then the survivor of a by-gone age. Her dark skirts hung as low as the tarpaulin which draped the mangle, and her skeletal shoulders were perpetually hunched beneath a woollen shawl. It was a mystery to me how they communicated, since neither was disposed to conversation. From George would come an occasional interrogative sound, which Annie either ignored or parried with interrogative noises of her own, neither facing the other.

They hadn't had much in the way of luck. As a girl, Annie had been put out to service, fetching and carrying for a previous Lime Street family. George, together with Annie and my grandfather, were orphaned before George's 10th birthday. According to my father, there still existed a sibling rivalry between George and my grandfather, though I never saw any evidence for it except that George was the younger by seven years and was expected, after all, to know his place.

George and Annie, rarely visiting or visited, were nevertheless part of the clan. My grandmother would cook for them while preparing a meal for those of her own family still at home. I was sometimes delegated to take a covered plate across the street to George's house. He had a healthy appetite for a man of his years, and ate his dessert with liberal helpings of bread and butter - either a local custom or a family idiosyncrasy, I never really discovered which.

In rare moments George would reminisce. He would recount a litany of events, disasters, anecdotes and opinions without thread or sequence and forget about them once utterance had been given. A recurring memory was of bar-house brawls in which he was involved and in which at least one of the belligerents was knocked through a plate glass window. It never occurred to me to ask how this feat was achieved, since the windows of The Railway Inn were at least four feet from floor level. Perhaps the brawlers were able to count levitation among their street-fighting skills.

His stories might have been apocryphal, but the flavour of a life lived for the moment, of pit-sweat and pay-packets intercepted by wives in wait by the pub door, remained with me long after I had left his house. But I never saw *George* leave the house. He and his sister seemed as fixed as the Tizer, the mangle and the nets between them. I made occasional explorative trips through the network of entries which encircled his terrace - some shoulder-wide, others the width of a handcart, some litter-strewn, others rain-washed to a blue sheen - and tried counting back gates to locate the entrance to the forbidden yard. It was something to do.

I thought on one occasion I had succeeded, only to find Vicar Cornes staring up at me as I peered over what I thought was George's gate. It was the vicarage I had found. We regarded each other for a moment, he in his robes, me with my collar askew, before a mute leave-taking.

I remember my grandfather's passing away, but not George's. All I have are snapshot memories of his eccentricities, his kindness, an endearing parochiality despite his service in the First World War and the frugality of his life. Like others of his era, he expected little and got it. England and Empire were synonymous in his eyes, and though he spent odd moments ranting against the lot of the poor and their rich oppressors, he believed to the end of his life that one Englishman was worth ten of anybody else.

Great Uncle George and Lime Street were swept away in the 1960s rush to redevelop, or to lay bare. But the memories are still there. And even now I can see the sun glinting on his bottle of Tizer and hear the occasional snap of his leather belt.

Grandad Harry Senior with Aunt Ivy in the Kent hop fields around 1935.

3. AN INTREPID VOYAGER

Great Uncle George never met my mother's father, Harry Senior. Harry was born in 1883 in Doncaster, but spent most of his life in a cramped terraced house in the gas-lit docklands of Deptford, East London. He was an adventurer by instinct, running away to sea at 13 and serving as a cabin boy on the last of the sailing vessels plying the continental sea lanes. Strong, square-jawed and resolute, he found the rigours of life on deck to his taste. He soon progressed to coastal freighters and the merchant ships which then formed the maritime backbone of the British Empire.

The hardships of his sea-going life, once mastered, only served to increase his thirst for fresh adventures. Within four years he had given up seafaring and, under-age and on impulse, decided to join the army. The reward for his impetuosity was a stint in the Boer War, where he served as a private.

Once the war was over, he returned to the Merchant Navy, this time working in a variety of jobs on the Cunard liners. In 1912 he was set on as a stoker aboard the SS White Star Liner, Titanic. He leapt clear before the ship went down and swam through the ice-cold waters to an already occupied boat. He tried several times to board it, but each time was knocked clear by survivors who were terrified lest he compromised their precarious safety. Eventually he managed to fight his way on board and was picked up by the liner Carpathia and taken to New York. He was one of the first to be interviewed by the American press and was able to provide descriptions of the scene on deck as the liner went down. Illustrations drawn from his narrative were used in the Illustrated London News.

Such a harrowing experience would have damaged a lesser man, but Harry took it in his stride. Two years later had signed on as able seaman on the Q Boats defending convoys in the North Atlantic during the Great War.

He returned to the Merchant Navy unscathed at the cessation of hostilities, leaving ship as the mood took him and pursuing his lust for life. At various times he was a cattle drover in South America, a bush ranger in Australia and a gold prospector in South Africa. He learned how to play mah jong in China and spent time in a Rio de Janeiro jail for being drunk and disorderly.

By the time he reached 40, he had sailed around the world many times. Finally he got the taste for travel out of fhis system and opted for a more secure life as a docker. His family, including my mother, was growing up, and their home and the docks were a stone's throw from each other.

However, the immense schoolboy humour which had driven his former daring refused to go away. A particularly memorable occasion found him on a tram going to the Elephant and Castle. None of the passengers noticed this thick-set working man take his seat at the tail of the vehicle and slip the catch off a couple of boxes he had brought with him. One of the boxes contained a snake - the exact species is not recorded - and the other a mongoose. How he came by either of these animals is not known, but my father, who told me what happened, vouched for this authenticity.

Harry awaited his chance and released both of them into the tram - with predictable results. Within minutes he had the tram to himself, while those among the passengers who had recovered from the shock summoned the nearest constable. Again my grandfather found himself a guest of the police and passed a night in a cell at Southwark.

Another incident had a similar result. Passing a police compound on his way from the pub he was somewhat surprised to find a huge grey mare facing him from the other side of a steel fence. The fence enclosed a police pound. Subject to the same old impulses, he decided to give the animal its freedom. He marched boldly into the compound and without more ado mounted the animal's back.

His house being close by, he was struck by the idea that merely stealing a police horse was an empty gesture. He might as well go the whole hog and inject a little excitement into the lives of his neighbours. Thus he came to treat the street to an impromptu display of his equestrian skills and continued to do so until its owners put in an appearance and escorted him on a now familiar journey - this time to Deptford Police Station.

Thus ran my grandfather's life throughout the 1920s and most of the 30s. He was still a strong, fearless man when he was diagnosed with cancer, and it was this rather than the wars, the Titanic and his travels throughout the world which eventually quelled the ardour which had burnt in him since youth. He died in 1937 aged 54.

4. HEALTH TO THE PEOPLE

One spoke the word "Doctor" in a hushed, reverential tone. He (never she) was the infallible dispenser of health to The People. The sight of his well-worn Gladstone put the colour back into your cheeks, or tempered it if the blush was due to fever.

Dr Halpin visited our house on numerous occasions in the forties and fifties. My father had served in the Metropolitan Police Force during the War. His Deptford beat suffered greatly from bombing raids, and he had been caught in the blast of an exploding V1 rocket as it demolished a row of houses. He was buried under the rubble, rescued and consequently spent some time in convalescence. Thereafter, he suffered with shrapnel wounds to the head and a lumbar weakness which it fell to Dr Halpin to treat.

Dr Halpin was indefatigable in his pursuit of good medicine and seemed to my childhood eyes an emblem of the newly-created National Health Service. I remember him balding, bespectacled and grinning, speaking in an unfamiliar accent, admitting himself with a curt-polite "Good Morning, Mrs Ridgway. Is he upstairs?" as he climbed unbidden to the bedroom. My father would undergo a perfunctory auscultation while Dr Halpin nodded sagely. "Mm... still something on the lung there." Returning his stethoscope to his bag, he would leave the bedside. "We'll see you on the mend. You must make sure he takes his tablets, Mrs Ridgway. And keep up with the fomentations. I'll see you again next week."

His surgery was an outbulding which nowadays deals in memorial stones. This might be mere coincidence, or maybe the two premises are an indication of the efficiency envisaged by Bevan when he set up his beloved health service. If "patch" or "dispatch" was indeed the touchstone of his policy, then that corner of Tunstall High Street can be held up as a shining example to all.

Patients occupied a bench which ran around the walls of the cramped waiting room. A door led to the surgery, guarded by a secretary whose job it was to hand you your medical card when your turn came. Order was dictated by your place on the benches, and as each patient left the waiting room those remaining shuffled ritualistically towards the vacated space. All this was carried out in lugubrious silence, and even at an early age the comedic possibilities were not lost on me.

I visited Dr Halpin with the usual childhood complaints. He occupied a small back-room containing the odd chart and sat in a Captain's chair set at an angle to his desk. On delivery of the diagnosis and prescription, you exited into a stableyard which opened on to the road. The system was a hallmark of post-war simplicity. Computer salesmen did not exist; the multi-phone lines, website and fax machines which nowadays keep an army of bureaucrats occupied were mercifully absent from his surgery. Like others of his time, he was wholly occupied in the job he was paid to do.

The shrapnel wounds my father had suffered 10 years earlier were no problem when they had healed. However, he was left with an intriguing egg-sized lump which protruded from his scalp despite his attempts to conceal it under an imaginative hair-style. Years later, and for no obvious reason, the lump decided to suppurate. It was Dr Halpin who volunteered a surgical solution. "Come down next week and we'll whip it off clean as a whistle." My father wondered whether living with his trade-mark lump would prove the lesser of two evils, but Dr Halpin's cheerful optimism dispelled any doubt.

The following week he presented himself after surgery hours. The practitioner swivelled around and, scalpel in hand, beamed at the lump with schoolboy enthusiasm. "Now you sit down here and we'll get started."

Hesitantly, my father sank into the seat. "This is not going to hurt, but you can hold on to the side if you want." My father gripped the chair, knuckles white as alabaster.

"Now, my beauty, we'll just make an incision to the side," the doctor said, addressing lump and scalpel simultaneously. He proceeded to slice through the growth, swabbing as he went. After a few seconds, and with an exclamation of delight, he dropped it into a basin which he then placed on the desk as if it were a sports trophy.

"That's the blighter. Now just press the wad to your head and I'll put a couple of stitches in it."

Such surgical feats were expected of GPs. Dr Halpin seemed to thrive on them, considering them perhaps a challenge or at least a more rewarding interval in the humdrum routine of coughs and colds.

I drove past what used to be his surgery recently. The memorial business is still going strong. There must be a lesson there somewhere.

5. TRAPS, CHURNS & AN ALVIS PICK-UP

No doubt Dr Halpin would have considered milk essential for a good diet. The milk trap called every day. It must have been one of the last of the horse-drawn deliveries, an anachronism even then. I remember collecting a quart from the milkman who ladled it from the churn into our container. I believe the man was a farmer by the name of Ellerton. It was the late 1940s or early '50s. His trap was big enough to hold a churn or two, a series of handled measuring jugs calibrated to half pints, pints and quarts and the milk-seller himself. A chestnut pony drew the trap, and was as conversant with the route and its stops as its owner.

The farmer-milkman was leisurely in his service and punctilious in his measures. Between doling out the milk and driving the trap he chatted inconsequentially to customers and allowed them to offer his pony a Cox's Orange Pippin, which it sometimes rejected with disdain.

While Mr Ellerton dealt with households in Chell Heath, Bradeley and Fegg Hayes, another gentleman catered for customers requiring a speedier service. This man was the antithesis of our home-drawn milkman in every way. Where Ellerton was slow, courteous and methodical, his rival dropped off the dailies at breakneck speed. Though he may have been inherently courteous, his appearances were too fleeting to provide evidence of it.

I have forgotten the man's name. I remember him as a middle-aged thickset local with collar-length hair and a perpetual coat. His claim to fame, and the reason why he was able to complete his rounds so quickly, was his Alvis pick-up. He seemed symbiotically attached to this vehicle. I can remember no occasion when he wasn't behind the wheel with his right foot to the ground.

The Alvis may have started its life as a car, but the conversion of vehicles from one role to another was commonplace at the time. The front section had status. The back end was merely a truck, but one which provided a climbing frame for the hordes of boys which accompanied him and who seemed anxious to help with the deliveries.

Where Mr Allerton still dealt from the churn, Alvis Man had moved on to bottles. These were crated at the rear and drunk by his numerous assistants over the course of the round. I noticed among the conventional pints odd-looking receptacles whose tops were attached to the glass with a spring steel hinge. The milkman was deterred neither by customer demands nor the state of the road. The unadopted and occasionally dangerous side streets off High Lane he would take at speed, his empties and the inevitable gaggle of lads rattling alike over the unmade surface. Housewives wishing to adjust their milk quota had little chance to make contact, though throughout the seasons the man's window was never up.

A third contestant for the local milk trade was the Co-op. They used electric vehicles, and the dairy was near Holden Lane. Instead of paying for the milk in cash, milk tokens were purchased from the Co-op store and left on the step to denote the quantity and type of milk required. A common feature was the miniature third of a pint bottles supplied to all schools and curtailed by Mrs Thatcher in the 1980s, I suspect at the behest of soft drinks companies.

I was once charged with delivering crates to a variety of schools. Later, as a teacher, I was responsible for seeing that the allocation was accurate. This was not as easy as it first appeared. Absenteeism often meant there were surplus bottles; who the beneficiaries of this extra milk would be was a lottery. In the early 1960s there still existed pockets of real deprivation and I tended to skew things so that the obviously malnourished would have first choice.

Before I left for college, I had a part-time job working for one of the large dairies. Electric floats were more economical than petrol-driven vehicles and have changed little in appearance since the 1950s. They had one shortcoming. If during the rounds the winter weather took a turn for the worse, they were in trouble. The weight of crates on the outward journey provided traction in moderate snow. However, as their load became progressively lighter, the wheels would begin to spin and the battery would drain. The result was the ignominy of having to be towed back to the depot by a petrol driven vehicle.

On more than one occasion I recall one of the older dairymen, on witnessing a midnight return of one of these towing vehicles, bemoan the passing of the horse-drawn drays of his youth. "They never 'ad any battery problems. And if you were new to a round th' 'oss'd show yer th' way."

6. MUSICAL SPOONS

Our local milkmen weren't the only characters. In an era of homogenised personalities, where the ad man's Never-Never Land is fed nightly through a million TV screens, I remember the less predictable personalities of my youth.

One individual in particular springs to mind. He made daily walking tours of our estate, always by the same route, always at the same measured pace and never for any discernible purpose. He looked 60 but could have been 20 years younger. Each excursion found him in an unbuttoned army trench coat and torn trousers narrowed to cycle-clip width at the ankle. His only shirt was grey with dirt and devoid of buttons; his soiled collar had the same bedraggled appearance as his oversize boots.

He wasn't a tramp - though he looked the part. He was known to have an address 'somewhere round the back', but no one knew exactly where. He would turn up at self-prescribed intervals and ply his rounds, an unlit butt clamped permanently between his lips, his cropped grey hair resistant to anything the weather might throw at it. Despite his briskness, he was careful at the road junctions, signalling right or left at each intersection. Many is the time he passed us with unseeing eyes, or at least eyes which only saw whatever he wanted them to see. Occasionally 'Buy a Colley' would be in the vicinity and their paths would cross. 'Buy a Colley' plied his trade from a handcart behind which a gang of urchins lurked, ready to thieve whatever lay within arm's reach. His skill was to exercise due politeness to prospective purchasers while berating the band of ruffians swinging from his cart. His attempts at civility on the one hand and reprimand on the other could prove unsettling, and on more than one occasion he left a bemused housewife to take a swipe at the nearest assailant.

His handcart was a cumbersome affair; that this diminutive purveyor of fruit and veg was able to haul it at all was little short of a miracle. Even more miraculous was his ability to make a profit, since the greater part of his merchandise had been filched well before he returned home.

Shorter even than "Buy a Colley", but equally swarthy, the Sentinel seller had a pitch in Tunstall High Street. While obvious deformity was becoming rarer by this time, evidence of physical disability was by no means uncommon. This newspaper seller had a withered leg and wore a high steel patten which clanked as he walked, sack in hand, from the Square to Pinnox Street. A stranger to the district would find the man's single utterance perplexing. To those in the know, however, "Tine-al" (drawn first syllable, accent on the second) could represent an eagerly awaited Stoke City result, a glimpse of local scandal or a third-hand Ford 'Pop'.

Other characters entered local folklore. Travelling from Tunstall to Mow Cop , the bus once picked up a group waiting at the Turnhurst stop. Among their number was a wizened individual in tweed cap and jacket, the sleeves of which stopped short of the wrist. More passengers got on at Packmoor and Harriseahead until the bus was almost full. On its final ascent, a voice from the back piped up: "Give us a turn on thee spoons, Ernie." I caught heads nodding and craned my neck to discover who the elusive Ernie could be. He of the shrunken sleeves was the answer, for without a second bidding he had removed a couple of tablespoons from an inner pocket and begun an impromptu recital. Before the bus reached its destination he had treated the company to a variety of effects in which his knees, hands and cutlery worked in perfect synchrony.

When the bus finally stopped he pocketed the spoons, briefly acknowledged the audience and departed. In an age of packaged eccentricities, the real thing would disturb the politically correct, who would no doubt have Ernie's musical spoons confiscated for his own good and Ernie himself delivered into the hands of Caring People.

Luckily, they are too late. So I say thank you to the Ernies of the world, wherever they may be, shrunken sleeves, spoons et al. They enriched my early life and will be fondly remembered long after other, more august personalities, have been forgotten.

PLACES

My early life was spent in and around the Potteries town of Tunstall, and it is inevitable that this once close-knit community, with its shops, cinemas, parks and streets, figure largely in my articles.

Throughout the 1940s and early 1950s I rarely ventured further than Tunstall - later Chell, where our new council house had been built. It was not long after this, however, that I was making occasional forays into Hanley, Smallthorne, Knypersley and even London.

Chapters

1. A Dolly in the Yard (Dec 1999)

2. Soda Suds & Reckitts Blue (Dec 1997)

3. Strictly for Visitors (April 2003)

4. A Medley of Bells (Sept 1998)

5. Wet Clay & Grit (April 2002)

6. Bulging Bags (August 1998)

7. Wonderland (October 1998)

8. A Day in the Park (May 1999)

9. Taking the Plunge (March 1999)

10. Ay Thanyew (March 1998)

11. I'll Get the Manager to Throw
You Out (June 2000)

1. A DOLLY IN THE YARD

I was a refugee from the London Blitz. My mother and I stayed with my father's sister in Pinnox Street, Tunstall, and after the war Sib and Lou put us up in their parlour rent free. We had no home of our own, and it was to be almost two years before our name moved to the top of the council house waiting lists.

My world was no bigger than a grain of sand. Yet that grain yielded the images of trains and buses, summer dusk and winter slush, encrustations of soot and the clank-clank of chains which came from mysterious sheds along the backs.

A viaduct spanned two streets and a timber yard. To my innocent eyes its arches seemed to be suspended from clouds that evolved into ghosts or galleons as I watched. I could hear the tankers' laboured snorts as the trains began their journey south from Tunstall Station. Moments later their rhythmic wheel-clicks would merge into an ominous rumble as the locomotive ran on to the viaduct. Ochre plumes met the grey, a cargo of crimson lake coaches pursuing the engine reluctantly around the curve.

I was fascinated by the sight of these trains in the sky, and would gaze in delight at their reflection in the parlour window as I stood on the ledge, pyjama clad, waiting for the bedtime call.

"Rumbling under blackened girders,
Midland, bound for Cricklewood,
Puffed its sulphur to the sunset
Where that Land of Laundries stood."

Cricklewood was 150 miles away, the only laundry I knew a dolly hanging from a nail in the yard. But those bursts of sulphurous steam against the red-bellied undercloud... yes, Betjeman had it right: Cricklewood and Pinnox Street had that in common at least.

One night I awoke to find my bedroom walls bathed in a fiery glow. Sparks leapt across the panes and there was a whiff of smoke in the air. I went to the window. Illuminated figures stood in huddled groups below. My mother was standing at the bedroom door. "Would you like to see the fire, Bill?"

Even before I got dressed I knew it was something to do with the viaduct. I expected to see a burning train and approached the open front door with mounting excitement. Chrome bright stars erupted from the parapet into the night sky. Scarlet shadows danced across the paling which enclosed the timber yard and ran up the viaduct brickwork. Flames were gushing from a spectral wagon which seemed to hover above the road. Apart from the crackle of fire, the night was uncannily hushed, the crowd motionless as the figures in a Lowry painting.

"If the wood yard goes up we're for it," I heard my mother say, as I hear her now, over 50 years later. But what happened next is lost to me, for I remember neither the fire being dowsed nor returning to my bedroom. The burning tableau still lingers in my mind as one of those persistent images you later discount as dreams. And the timber yard -White and Taylor, I think it was called - survived to continue its business for many years.

Close to the viaduct, and opposite my aunt's house, stood a dilapidated hall which predated the terraces which enclosed it. Its grandeur had suffered an ignominious blight from kiln smoke and belching chimneys, yet it had managed to retain something of its former dignity. It was a testament to the preindustrial age, before the advent of railways and coal and the terraces which housed those who worked in and for them.

Perhaps it was a remnant of Georgian England, when fields, not factories were the predominant feature. I would look up at its opaque windows and down the litter-strewn basement steps before returning quickly across the road to the safety of our parlour.

An alley separated my aunt's back yard from a tract of sheds and sidings. The alley was of cart width, a mixture of shard, conglomerate and vitiated soil through which tufts of grey grass struggled. The nearest line was part of a higgledy-piggledy maze which ran off the Whitfield mineral route and served a couple of local firms. The tracks were uneven, the shunters chugging like ponderous beetles from point to point for reasons of which I was oblivious.

One day, a friend and I decided to see what would happen to a coin placed in a shunter's path. We spotted our chance and crawled through the broken fencing. I fumbled an old penny out of my pocket. The tarnished face of George V gazed up at me. A quirk of malice caused me to place the coin Britannia down, so that the monarch's profile would receive the wheels' full impact. We hid as the locomotive rumbled towards, then over the illustrious visage. Once the last wisps of steam had cleared, we went to inspect the damage. The coin had expanded, the proud moustache and noble forehead squashed to a democratic pancake.

Thus ended George, unspent and later discarded in the Pinnox Street backs, an unwilling metaphor for the empire which in the late 1940s was drawing ineluctably to its close.

Lime Street, Tunstall: a place for family get-togethers.
I'm on the sill with cousin Pat. Grandma Ridgway is
taking no chances.

2. SODA SUDS & RECKITT'S BLUE

Lime Street, the home of my grandparents, was a stone's throw from my aunt's house and my visits to Lime Street were frequent.

I try to remember a time when my grandfather moved from his chair, but cannot. He seemed as fixed as the grandmother clock, the inherited chaise longue, the bun-legged table and the traps Grandma set for those mice foolhardy enough to climb the cellar steps as Lime Street slept. His cardiganed back to the yard window, he would sit for hours tamping his twist and gazing through the faded wallpaper. Grandma, on the other hand, bustled through her days in a foam of soda suds and Reckitt's Blue.

My father's family had lived in Tunstall for three generations. Lime Street was one of many to the west of the Square which had absorbed our diaspora. The street was linked to adjacent thoroughfares by a network of blue-brick entries strewn with half-enders and dead cats. The pub stood opposite St Mary's vicarage at one end, there was an oatcake shop at the other, and, mid-way between the two, a coal yard heaped with uncarted sacks.

The War Office decreed that air-raid shelters be strategically located, on the premise that there was less chance of being killed as a result of enemy action if the local populace were crammed into a single concrete block. Lime Street's shelter smelled of cats' pee and soot. By the time the Victory street parties took place, the entrances had been bricked up prior to its demolition.

There was no future in clay, so my father left Platt's brickyard in the early Thirties and joined the Metropolitan Police Force in London. My mother lived on his Deptford beat. They were married three years before war broke out. By the time I was bom in 1940 we had moved to Greenwich, away from the terraces abutting the heavily bombed docks and sugar warehouses which lined the river.

Snapshot memories remain; of the flooded Anderson shelter at the bottom of our garden, the drone of bombers and the searchlights sweeping up from Greenwich Park. As the situation deteriorated, my mother and I caught the evening train at Euston. I slept my way to Stoke while my father remained in London. My early years seem to have been spent in dimly-lit compartments packed with smoking squaddies, their impedimenta stacked precariously above railway pictures of Rhyl.

We lodged with my grandparents in the safer precincts of Lime Street until 1944, when my father was invalided out of the Force. When war ended we went to stay with my father's sister and her family at Pinnox Street. By then an addition to the family in the form of my brother had arrived, and the four of us shared a spartan parlour.

My father was in no state to work, but he had a family to support. The problem of space was pressing. Though my aunt and uncle couldn't have been more accommodating, the domestic situation was far from ideal. For a time my father found employment as a painter for Brundett's, but the job, which involved red-leading ironwork from a bosun's chair, would never be eagerly anticipated by a man with no head for heights.

One day in 1946 the postman dropped an official letter through the door. I was playing in the corner with an aluminium-painted boat my uncle had made me and was too engrossed at first to hear my mother's shout of jubilation. We had been granted a council house. A house of our own. As a child of six, this seminal information passed me by. But the next weekend my mother push-chaired my brother and coaxed me the mile and a half to Sprink Bank to view Plot 54, on which a pair of semis were in the course of erection. She pushed her way through builders' rubble as far as the criss-cross struts protecting the doorway and peered through the unglazed window.

"Wait till I tell your Dad." She spoke in an incongruous Cockney accent, nowadays diluted with the passing years. I looked around. Friesians were grazing adjacent plots. From below the rise came the clank of pit wagons and the soft chuffing of a locomotive.

"That's Whitfield," she said. "Where they get the coal from."

We moved in the Autumn of that year. I changed schools, this time to Chell, where I was taught by a long-necked schoolmaster with a prominent Adam's apple nick-named Polly Rubberneck, and a music teacher who encouraged us to sing a gusty *Men of Harlech* with the aid of a plimsoll.

At nine I moved again, this time to a newly-built primary school in Chell Heath where I painted in the sunshine, played the *Tales of Hoffman* at the Christmas Concert and out-ran the den-keeper in games of Rally-O. My first girlfriend Christina furnished me with daily liquorice as a token of her undying love and the plaited Joan Mayer was invited by Miss Martin, our teacher, to entertain us on the violin with her Gilbert and Sullivan favourites.

It was about this time that a friend of someone on the estate parked his new Standard Vanguard ostentatiously amid a group of admiring neighbours. And then that I had my first brush with 'Buy a Colley' whose grocery cart provided sustenance and entertainment to pillagers bent on food and fun.

Grandad Ridgway 'as fixed as the grandmother clock'.

3. STRICTLY FOR VISITORS

Although we had settled into our new council house, my grandfather's Lime Street home was still the place for family get-togethers. The street was one of a network of thoroughfares huddled on the fringes of Tunstall between the shard-strewn remains of Bradwell Wood and the Square.

Smith Child's clock, situated where the old Stun House once stood, marked the high point of a Pennine ridge whose slopes fell towards Greenbank Road in the east and the canal in the west. The valley through which the canal, and later the railway, were built, must at one time have been as beautiful as any in the country. The sprawl of industry ousted all but remnants of the valley's former state, and by the early 19th century, pot banks, churches, pubs, terraces and tileries had encroached on anything still growing on the slopes.

Workers came from peripheral villages and moved from other parts of the growing city to be where the work was. Close-knit societies formed based on the street, more loosely on an undefined locality. My grandfather lived in one such canton, those in the 'posher' areas around Stanley Street in the east, to another. In my youth, terrace and territoriality were much the same, with the totemic pub, church, shop, priest, teacher and occasional troublesome family providing the local reference points. There was always an 'Ena Sharples' character to hand, incense on Sundays and the plock of a skittles' ball just audible through the open doorway of the pub.

All this went in the 1960s. Along with the demolition of the houses south of Nash Peake Street and west of Ladywell came the extirpation of shared experience and the security of familiar faces. A root of the tree of English society had been hacked off and no amount of plaster would stick it on again. My grandfather's house went with the rest, the foundations no doubt used as hardcore for the primary school which later rose from the rubble.

Lime Street and other similar terraces in the area were among the first to be built in Tunstall. I believe some dated back to the 1840s, and although water now came from a tap, rather than a pump, the structures were quite capable, with renovation, of on-going accommodation as in other parts of this and other cities. My grandfather's house was, like the rest, modest. One stepped through the front door to a cramped, tiled, parlour. Set in one wall was a fireplace, in another a sash window opening onto the street. A settee and easy chair occupied much of the space, together with a display cabinet containing ceramic figures and the 'best china'. My grandmother insisted you use the hessian mat as you stepped in, not the rag rug which lapped the castors.

The parlour was strictly for visitors, particularly the vicar and others who might drop in after the Sunday service. These more or less illustrious people were kept out of the living room. No 'best china' there, nor figurines either. A blanket-covered chaise longue stood close to the range, the range itself flanked by capacious floor-to-ceiling cupboards. What these cupboards contained was a mystery to me, as it probably was to the occupants of the house too, since I never saw the doors open and wasn't sufficiently curious to discover the contents myself.

My grandmother sometimes black-leaded the range, so that in a certain light the words Baxendale and Co, Manchester, stood out in glistening threads against the hob. It seemed to me that the fire was always stoked up, that no one was ever seen stoking it, and that its main function was to receive dottle from my grandfather's pipe.

Another sash overlooked a blue-brick yard. Beneath this window a bun-legged table and a chair containing my permanently puffing granddad resided. Since he rarely spoke, the only sounds were the soft plop of falling coal and the soporific tick-tock-tick of the wall clock above his head.

The living room led into the scullery. This was the demotic part of the house, from which ironed shirts and potato pies issued. Had the vicar by accident ventured there, my grandmother would have offered up prayers for universal salvation. For here was stored the paraphernalia of wash day, the dolly in the galvanised tub, a couple of wash boards, a brick-sheathed corner boiler and a rickety wooden table scrubbed white over the years.

The large sink was of brown pitcher. A single cold tap fed the sink, the laundry, the various dull steel saucepans which occupied a shelf above a gas cooker and the bucket for slopping down the brick floor. The scullery ended in a yet smaller room, which contained coal.

You had to pass through these rooms to reach the outdoor toilet. This had been built as a seeming afterthought at the end of the yard, and consisted of a plank with a hole. The torn remains of *Sentinels* were to be found wedged behind the water inlet. No one chose to go there after the Sunday service. Certainly not the vicar. My grandmother would have been mortified.

4. A MEDLEY OF BELLS

Sundays have changed. From my window I could hear a medley of bells calling the Faithful to service. The air rang with notes whose cadence filled the texture of Sabbath life as much as Sunday Roast, Family Favourites and the essential lie-in.

We would walk with my father to Tunstall, the peals strengthening as we neared the mineral line which crossed Little Chell Lane. They crescendoed as we made our way along Victoria Park Road to Station Road, hence to the Square and on to Lime Street. We saw neither bus nor car on our journey into town, and those on foot could be counted on one hand.

Sunday quiet was unlike any other. No common tranquillity, but an indefinable air of peace enveloped the town. One was at ease with oneself. Sunday was a totem which marked the end of the working week, an oasis in the bustle of everyday life. One recharged oneself for the days ahead. Sunday represented balm and order, security amid strife.

We attended St Mary's Church. It stood in its Gothic glory, pointing a sooty finger at the Lime Street skies and calling sinners to repentance. We gathered with family and friends in the parlour of my grandmother's house before making our way through the iron railings which excluded all but True Christians. A figure of the crucified Christ occupied a niche between abutments; as a child I always cast a sideways look in His direction, to make sure I was following the Path.

Vicar Cornes seemed at once remote and austere. He officiated over a cavernous interior sprinkled with lights from the stained glass windows. His sermons were full of references to The Blood of Christ and The Lamb and I seemed to find lurid echoes of his words under those Gothic arches. The windows' vivid colours fascinated me. Gaudily Pre-Raphaelite, they seemed to enshrine all that was sacred in Sunday worship. After the service we would return to my grandmother's house. I would make myself scarce while the adults enjoyed one of those Sunday get-togethers that were convivial and spiritual in equal measure.

My father told me that Bradwell Wood was all that remained of the Forest of Lyme from which Newcastle derived its name and which at one time covered huge tracts of the Midlands. We often went there after the crowd at my grandmother's had dispersed. Even then, in the early Fifties, it was a shadow of what it must have been. The detritus of past activity spilled into the hawthorn, shardy lanes led to overgrown adits and the skeletons of winding houses reared against the sky.

But it was not all like that. Here and there existed small woodland glades which by accident had survived the surrounding dereliction. One then had a sense of what was once taken for granted, before the land yielded its clay and coal to those who built the encroaching city.

I remember cold Sundays in April, when the pussy willows speckled the extinct tileries in white fluff, and the remnants of blackthorn hedges powdered the tracks. And May, when the musk of bluebells scented the air and dense campion clumps took root by rust-coloured runnels. Drifts of wood sorrel clouded the copses of stunted birch and, on the margins of clay, yellow carpets of celandine grew. In spring, nature pulled a green blanket over the tips and adits, over the shardrucks and cast-off railings.

It was not hard to imagine yourself back a hundred years and a hundred miles from Tunstall Market Square, but 10 minutes away up the riggot. And the only sound the continuous, lilting larksong which came from the canopy of leaves.

A child was a child at that time, not a pretend adult in bomber and jeans. The land was mystical. Hobgoblins lived under hawthorn roots and if you took the wrong track you would end up in the witch's cauldron. Hideous faces leered from the bark of trees, green faces peeped from the leaves and breezes wafted the chill of far-off lands into the copses where we sheltered from the showers.

I once saw the remains of a tiled floor in the undergrowth. "Used to be a gamekeeper's house," my father told me. I could imagine the ghost of Mellors stepping over the threshold in his shirtsleeves and waistcoat. Maybe Lady Chatterley was hanging around outside one of the old winding towers, looking impatiently at her watch.

With the advent of cheap motoring, the Sundays I knew vanished. Church bells now constitute noise abuse. It is many years since St Mary's was demolished. And there's a road where the skylarks used to sing.

5. WET CLAY & GRIT

The A500 cuts through the remains of Bradwell Wood near the site of my grandmother's old home. The land here was littered with the detritus of former industrial activity. The end of Lime Street marked the beginning of a parallel world, one inhabited by the ghosts and goblins of another age. They lived in the remnants of Bradwell Wood, which still asserted itself in pockets of hazel and rowan. The ghosts were those of former workers, the miners and quarrymen who had spent their lives feeding a Victorian appetite for power and production.

St Mary's was closer to heaven than the brick-kilns which surrounded it. A shardy path close by the church led to Platt's brickyard, time-warped even in the 1950s. China-strewn ground, muddy in winter, dusty in summer, gave access to a range of dilapidated sheds and kilns. The air tasted of grit and wet clay. Nothing grew. Church, school and brickyard were strangely united, the survivors of earlier times, comforting but austere. A rough track led downwards to the canal and railway line. It was known as the Riggot. Steel troughs had at some time been set at its edge. My grandfather told me they were to guide carts up the hill and make the work of the drays easier. I suspect the real purpose was more mundane; the tramps made a gutter so that the track, already cratered and precarious, wouldn't be washed away.

At one side of the track, and occupying much of its length, was a water-filled marl hole. To my childhood eyes, it was shrouded in mystery. According to folklore, this was the site of many calamities, of hapless swimmers sucked to a watery doom, of cramps and undefined weeds against which even the strongest swimmer was helpless. Its sides rose sheer from the water. The flimsy fence which surrounded it was patched and broken. Ghostly sirens wailed as I passed. I closed my ears to their enticements and quickened my pace.

At the bottom of the Riggot, unused railway lines sprang from the mud. Once I came across a rail cart still on the tracks. I pushed it down the line and sprang on board while the momentum lasted. The cart was heavier than it looked, and my exertions soon proved futile. I left it on the points. Maybe it's still there, forever awaiting another passenger.

Between the tracks and the canal was a bargees' pub; opposite, on the other side of the canal, a short row of terraced houses. Both pub and cottages could have been a hundred miles from the hubbub of Tunstall High Street, less than 10 minutes' walk up the Riggot. Even then, it was difficult to see how the landlord made a living, since the only person ever to take a drink there seemed to be my father. There must have been many publicans who were equally grateful to my father for his practical concern for their livelihood.

Through the margins of the wood ran the main railway line. The land undulated unnaturally, each mound, ditch and track betraying some former activity. Broken teapots lay half buried in the clay. Stunted birches grew through the pyramids of broken tiles. Here the unwary could be tripped by a cable, slip unnoticed down an adit or plunge to his death down some long forgotten drain. Perilous walls reared from the grass, cowlings and girders thrust through the blackberries and occasionally a vast, industrial monument would spring from the waste.

I remember one building, a cavernous, roofless structure whose ghosts had presided over the encroaching dereliction for a century. Was it the remains of a winding house? What purpose had it served? When was it last used and who were the users? I used to climb through a doorway, now raised above the surrounding land, into a Roman forum or a ruined Gothic hall. A hundred years of rain had trailed rusty encrustations down the brickwork. The windows, some with their iron lattices still intact, looked out on a bright sky. Ferns grew in dank corners. Banks of earth formed the floor. In one part a row of steps ended in tumbled brick and charred timber struts. Pigeons cooed above my head. Bonsai shrubs grew from soil-less clefts and pockets. I couldn't stick it for long, but the fascination always drew me back.

Unlike this decaying testament to old mines, Goldendale iron works was still in full swing. My father took me once to watch pig-iron being made. It was said to be the finest pig-iron in Staffordshire, if not the entire world. A mound now marks the spot where the iron works used to be.

My Gothic mansion has long since gone, as have the rail sidings and the lukewarm shandies my father treated me to as a child at the bargees' pub. The canalside terrace is still there, a last defiant symbol of a vanished world.

6. BULGING BAGS

It would be some years before the superstores cornered the bulk of the trade in the Potteries. The mainstay of business in Tunstall in the decade after the war was the family shop. Shopping was still an expedition, and prior to the widespread use of cars bulging bags had to be manhandled home. Few people had refrigerators; meat bought in the summer had to be quickly consumed or left to the maggots.

My mother made the one mile journey to the shops by bus several times a week. She did the bulk of her food shopping at Frank Danby's. Frank ran a small High Street grocery below the Market Square and represented an archetypal grocer of the time. Professionally neither glum nor pushy, he served with a customer-is-always-right panache six days a week behind a counter festooned with cans and bottles.

Entering Frank's emporium was like stepping into an Aladdin's cave of comestibles. Every space was occupied, every niche and shelf stocked to the gunnels with tins, packs, jars and crates. I was awe-struck by his cheeses. Apart from the handy, cut, varieties, he always had knee-high Cheddar cylinders clad in muslin and occupying pride of place behind the counter. You would have expected them to stink, but they didn't; or at least any smell was neutralised by the medley of other odours which swirled around his cramped quarters.

"Yes, Mrs Ridgway, and what will you have today?"

"Hello, Frank. I'd better start with a couple of pounds of sugar."

Frank would tip the sugar into a brown paper bag; almost everything in that non-pre-packed era was handled likewise.

Ben Mallinder's was situated almost opposite Frank Danby's. His speciality was bikes, but he also sold radios and light bulbs. I had my first new bike from Ben, a sit-up-and-beg Raleigh with an oil bath around the chain and an electric dynamo powering lights fit to blind.

And it was from Ben that my father had our first accumulator-free radio. In the early Fifties our new Bush was as state-of-the-art as you could buy. On getting it home, my father spent an hour adjusting the frequency to a variety of Continental radio stations, just to enjoy its undistorted tones.

Sited on the south side of the Market Square, the Home and Colonial was famed for its whizzing cash boxes. My aunt worked there, in a sort of glass kiosk whose purpose seemed to be to control the boxes as they sped from the counter. My mother called there for the few things she was unable to acquire at Frank Danby's and my father called there to pass the time of day with Dorothy.

The Home and Colonial seemed swish compared to Frank's. Its name was depicted in impressive gold letters, and the inside was uncluttered and spacious. Looking back, I suppose it pointed to the changes that would revolutionise the retail trade a few years later.

The hub of the town was Tunstall Market. Uniquely pervaded by smells and an echoing bustle you could find nowhere else, the market seemed to ensnare a continuity of time. I shopped there as a small child in the mid Forties and on occasions over the next 40 years. The atmosphere never changed during that time, and I have no reason to believe it was substantially different in the 19th century when the town dignitaries set up stalls in honour of Victoria's Jubilee. Here my mother purchased brisket and oranges and, later, my wife bought oddments from the haberdashery stall.

For some years the market was in a sorry state. I fail to understand the myopia of those who let such gems disintegrate. Or perhaps its popularity would have whisked the precious purchaser away from the characterless shopping centre in Hanley, for which another equally bustling market was sacrificed? Thankfully Tunstall market was saved at the eleventh hour and will survive to enhance the town.

Tunstall then was a vibrant town, and it served the northern end of the city well. It was, and is perhaps still, a village within a city, bounded by its Market Square clock on one hand and its park on the other, by its church to the north and the old brickyard to the south where my great grandfather died of heart disease at the age of 42.

It holds many memories for me; of Easter Parades and the occasional lumbering dray; of a die-cast car given me as a present and lost the same day in Tunstall Park; of Barber's Picture Palace and Keen's; of early romances and the measured strike of hob-nails against the blue-brick at the end of a shift.

Give or take a handful of terrace streets, it remains in essence as it was. But the communality of that time has been lost. Frank would know what I was talking about.

7. WONDERLAND

In the Forties and Fifties, the Potteries could boast a cinema on every street. Well, almost. I must have visited most of them at one time or another during my early teens. Some were monumental Art-Deco palaces, attended by commissionaires as conspicuously attired as the captains of a South American liberation army. Others were back-street bug-huts whose projection beams assailed the heads of usherette and customer alike - while the customers assailed the actors with a variety of contemptuous sounds, ranging from a mock kiss to a ribald comment at an appropriate place in the inevitable B movie.

Tunstall had three cinemas: Barber's Picture Palace in what was then Station Road, its smaller brother the Regent Picture Hall off Haymarket and The Ritz in the High Street. My favourite was the Picture Palace, but I was also a frequent visitor to the Ritz, where they ran a popular Chums' Club on Saturday mornings. I can only remember going to the Haymarket cinema once, to see a Laurel and Hardy film with the duo in a runaway big-dipper car.

A visit to the cinema was a visit to wonderland. One dressed up to go there. You joined an orderly, if expectant queue and waited in the rain to be told there were no more shilling seats left. One left behind the gloom of the city for dimmed lights and a vanilla tub, the almost inaudible swish of velvet curtains and two hours of fantasy, Hollywood style. You left the ovens and kilns to their own devices. Cinema was a sanctum, a womb to escape the rigours of the street. The orchestra would strike, the audience would still, out would come the Cadbury's and on the screen would flash the credits in glorious Technicolor.

I met them all at Barber's Picture Palace. I was introduced to Chopin in the form of Cornel Wilde and to Laurence Olivier's Heathcliff. When I forgot the rustle of sweet bags, I would sail the isthmus of Panama with Columbus and tearfully watch Bambi's dad die in the forest fire. I joined Maxim de Winter at the wheel of his car and Mrs Danvers at her burning window. We spilled out after the Anthem and caught the bus, pursued all the way home to Chell by the ghosts of the silver screen.

At Barber's Picture Palace you purchased a disc which you handed to the usherette before entering the auditorium. Buying a ticket at The Ritz was more conventional. The Ritz was much bigger than the Palace, a labyrinthine building full of secret rooms and passages resplendent with photos of the Hollywood Greats.

But it was long past its heyday even then. An air of faded grandeur lingered in the passages. Glitzy colour schemes, the pinks and the mauves of walls painted long ago, now looked tatty. Diamond-toothed stars had nothing to smirk about; they presided over stained carpets, ripped couches and lights dimmed not to illuminate the atmosphere, but to prevent you from seeing it. Still, like Barber's, it retained something of its former magic when the curtains opened and the ranks of silhouetted heads coupled or parted beneath the beam.

I doubt we noticed much of the decor at the Chums' Club, which was marked by the exuberance of its regulars and the rigour with which they scorned The Baddie. And there were plenty of baddies, easily recognised by their predilection for black. The good cowboy wore a white hat, the loathsome outlaw black. The avenging angel sported a silver suit, his sinister counterpart stroked a cat. The cat was black, and as sinister as its owner.

One episode ended with the car plunging over the cliff, the good guy at the wheel. A week later and he was three hundred yards from the drop and driving like Stirling Moss in the opposite direction. The beautiful girl was blonde and fleshy. She was a good girl really, just misled.

For years I could not pass Barber's crumbling facade or the entrance to what used to be The Ritz without seeing Ali Baba, his oiled pecks full of eastern promise. Or listening to the strains of remembered voices whispering: "I cannot live without my life! I cannot die without my soul!" .... "Why don't you leave Mandalay? He doesn't need you. He has his memories."   ....."That's another fine mess you've gotten me into......."

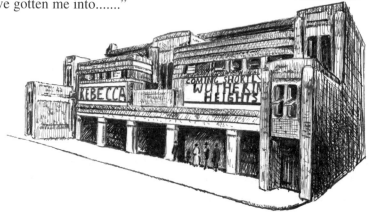

8. A DAY IN THE PARK

The Victorians who envisaged the city's many parks had different sorts of entertainment in mind. Parks provided an essential lung for the townships they served and helped mitigate the industrial pall which had sullied the air for decades. Like the surrounding towns, each park nurtured an individuality which was nevertheless cohesive in terms of its formal prettiness and common purpose. They were built within a few years of each other, and encapsulated the prevailing ideal of health, leisure and exercise for the masses.

I was a frequent visitor to Tunstall Park in the Forties and Fifties. It had changed little since it was first laid out on cinder beds early in the century. Although most of the principal features remain, it is not as popular as it once was. As cars became common, their owners grew more adventurous and headed east to the Peak District or west to the Cheshire countryside in their free time. By the late Sixties the park had relinquished its majority stake in the lives of those it was designed to serve, but it never entirely capitulated.

When we were children, my mother often took my brother and me to the children's playground. At that time it was situated alongside the mineral line which carried the coal trains from Whitfield to Longport. Before the age of health and safety, it boasted a feast of traps for the unwary. Close by the boundary were two slides, one for infants, the other for seasoned adventurers. We always made a bee-line for the taller of the two and slid down its brass-plated chute in a variety of inelegant positions. Merely mounting the 30 steps to the top was proof of manhood. One surveyed those on the ground with a haughty disdain before going down backwards, face to the sky.

Even more lethal was a device which resembled a giant cone with wooden seats attached to the outside. Encouraged by its hordes of foot-kicking passengers, the cone would revolve haphazardly on a lofty spindle, throwing newcomers across the slabs with careless abandon. Anyone fortunate enough to have kept his grip on the bars would soon envy those hurled away when the first sensations of nausea tickled his tummy.

The swing boat did almost as good a job in unsettling the stomach. Several boats were attached to a towering framework and worked by a central lever pulled by opposing sitters. As the tugs grew faster and more frenetic, so the boats rose higher and arced wider. A true practitioner could coax his boat into the near-vertical, both partners pinned to their seats by prayer and centrifugal force. There were no seat belts; lawyers were yet to invent the notion of safety. Even the boat sides had been pared to a minimum, a triumph of economics over imagination.

The Conservatory held the same arcane fascination for me as the railway station, a few hundred yards beyond the park gates. The minute you opened the door an evocative mix of scents wafted up from tiers of exotic plants. The air was equatorial, the slabbed floor shiny with spray water and moss. There was a single path linking doors at either end of the structure. Dappled with fern shade and overhanging bloom, the path to me was secret, detached from the outside world by mysterious botanical forces beyond my control. It abutted the Floral Hall, home to receptions and betrothals, meetings and festivals and at one time in constant use. As was the larger of the two lakes where, for a few pence, a boat could be hired.

On summer Sundays, all the boats would be on the water. It was one man's job to collect the money and procure the vessel, and, yes, he really did shout "Boat number three, your time is up," or something of the kind to youths who took no notice.

I went out on the boats more than once, and was witness to a rich variety of boating styles. I remember one with poignant clarity. The rower must have tired of conventional oarsmanship and decided on a novel technique for getting his boat back to the boat house: standing in the stern and propelling the craft with a single oar, canoe-style. The boat seemed quite responsive to his skill - unlike a swan which obstinately refused to clear the way. This threw the oarsman, both metaphorically and physically. He made an attempt to retain his standing position, but his talent was not quite up to it. The last I saw of him he was wading towards the boat house, his boat in tow. I didn't realise until then the extent of the boatkeeper's vocabulary.

The clock tower is still there, and the glacial boulder we slid down as children. The flag tower, once a skating rink, is now in a sorry state. The paddling pool which was once situated at its foot has been filled in. The Floral Hall is just a memory.

Yet the park still retains a provincial charm and remains a credit to those who created it almost a century ago.

9. TAKING THE PLUNGE

Cycling and swimming also occupied my leisure hours in the early 1950s. For a while swimming was my main pastime. I went with friends, either to Tunstall or Burslem baths.

Both must have represented the pride of Victorian weal when they were built. In the 1950s they were in their original state and you didn't need to be over-endowed with imagination to see Captain Webb emerging from one of the cubicles. The water level was a couple of feet below the side, and the sides and base were plainly tiled in the utilitarian manner of municipal buildings.

It was also possible to have a hot private bath for a small fee. The surrounding terraces lacked modern plumbing and many who attended were non-swimmers who paid their dues for something more than a galvanised tin in front of the hearth.

The cubicles demonstrated the prudery of the Victorians towards all things naked. They were ranked alongside the pool and you were expected to change behind a door which bolted.

Burslem had a diving stage at the "deep end" - which was rarely more than five and a half feet. Accidents were a natural consequence and the diving stage was eventually removed, having witnessed weekly abrasions for the better part of 80 years without comment. The diving stage had three fixed tiers. The top stage was about seven feet from the water and it was while making near-vertical descents from this that over-zealous divers came to grief.

At the time I attended a youth club in Macclesfield Street, Burslem. There was never anyone in charge as far as I can remember, and an obligatory game of table tennis was meant to keep us off the street. For a fearless character named Mac, however, the delights of ping pong were insufficient. He craved greater indulgences, and suggested to me that we pay a visit to Burslem Baths the following Saturday, where I would see him perform an unrivalled feat of daring. I quickly agreed to meet him by the pool.

He turned up at 11.00 clutching his towel and a pair of trunks which could have been put to better use cleaning the boiler. We paid our money and by the time I had emerged from my cubicle Mac was already in the water.

After going through the various routines of diving through each others legs and retrieving a threepenny bit from the deep end, I asked Mac to show me his feat. I don't think verrucae were widespread at that time. Nevertheless Mac obliged. "No Mac. I mean your *feat.* That doffer you were telling me about." His frown faded and he gave a beam of understanding. Without further ado he heaved himself out of the water and made his way to the far end of the pool.

The baths, like the youth club, was conspicuously free of attendants. Mac noted this and immediately climbed on to the diving stage. From the third tier it was possible for a man to reach a bracing timber which spanned the rafters. Mac was short and lean as a skinned rabbit. A single spring, and he had the strut in both hands. With a sinuous movement he levered himself up. Straddling the beam, he gave vent to a full-throated Johnny Weismuller cry, rose to his feet and proceeded to walk across it until he was poised over the water. No one seemed particularly impressed. Maybe Mac did this sort of thing every day. I couldn't take my eyes off him, and he focused his attention on me.

"Watch this!" He now favoured a Sioux war-whoop, and, as he was giving it, dived steeply into the deep end. It was some time before he emerged, his ebullience quelled and sporting an egg-sized lump above the temple. What could I say? Mac found the words, most of them expletives. According to him, his mishap had a variety of causes - including myself. "I can't do it right when people are looking."

"Are you surprised?" I asked.

"I'm off home. I've got to go somewhere." He departed. I never saw him at the youth club after that, nor at the baths. I suppose he's still about somewhere, looking for more beams to climb. Paragliding or bungee jumping, perhaps.

He certainly won't be performing his stunts at Burslem Baths, since they no longer exist.

10. AY THANYEW

It didn't take us long to settle into our Chell home and for my father to find a new local. His hobby was exercised in the late Forties in frequent visits to the local Workingmen's Club. His forays were usually unaccompanied, but on Saturday nights we would go along too.

The word 'club' held an arcane fascination for me. Pubs were off-limits to nine year olds, yet a club could fling wide its doors and welcome a swaddling infant if accompanied by a Responsible Adult. Why? I could make no sense of it, but the anticipation of its illicit attractions held me in thrall.

The club had once been a large farmhouse, and at that time retained a pastoral ambience. Its grounds had been made into a bowling green and dense aucuba thickets hid yelling broods of customers' children, of which I was one. As dusk came on, we would disentangle ourselves from the shrubbery and, together with the last of the bowlers, go inside to join our parents.

A narrow flight of stairs led to the principle room. Here 'turns' were performed by the more bibulous of the patrons who by nine o'clock had acquired not only a significant Dutch courage, but the unyielding conviction they were a Richard Tauber waiting to be discovered.

Ike presided over the artistes from a chair below the dais. He had a cauliflower ear and wore black horn-rimmed glasses. Ike was the Master of Ceremonies and of an Arthur Askey-type delivery whereby "All right, ladies and gentlemen, I thank you," (for keeping quiet during the act) was reduced to "Arite ladgentman, ay thanyew." If the audience remained seditious, he reinforced his pleas by violently ringing an electric bell and exhorting us to "Order, please. Order. Ay thanyew." The pianist was a plump, middle-aged woman known as Beatie whose face betrayed no hint of emotion whatever the voice she was called upon to accompany.

I only heard my father sing once. Beatie gazed with glorious intransigence at the piano lid while Ike struggled with the crowd. "Order. Order." Two rings. "Order!" His knuckle-white smile grew more menacing and he faced his charges with the feinting stance of a retired welter-weight. "Arite ladgentman, ay thanyew."

Eventually silence reigned and Beatie struck an introductory chord.

Spying his advantage, Ike cut in: "Bill's gointa sin' for us. *River Stay Way from my Door.*"

My mother sipped her 'gin and it' and gazed stonily through the window. My father fixed his eye on the far wall and began: "I ain't goin' yo way, yo ain't goin' ma way, river, stay 'way from ma door....." He sang in the dolorous tones of an Alabama minstrel, making vast chunks up as he went along, occasionally incorporating snatches of other songs. As Beatie struck the final chords the room erupted in applause. But the next performer was in the wings, and Ike's voice had already risen above the din. "Rite, ay thanyew. Order. Order. ORDER!"

One of the advantages of regular attendance at the Club was your entitlement to an annual trip. I suppose I was nine or ten when, with mounting excitement and a regulation pack of sandwiches, we crocodiled down to Pittshill station to await the train to Rhyl. The early haze had dispersed to reveal a fine day. We were done up in our best, gartered socks taut, short trousers newly pressed, shoes burnished mirror-bright. A distant hoot from Tunstall Station raised our excitement to fever-pitch. Within minutes a soot-blackened locomotive hove into view, the driver leaning out of his cab with studied disinterest. We were still scrambling for space in our chosen compartment as the train moved slowly out.

"We're off, off, off in a motor car,

Twenty cops are after us and don't know where we are."

"Open the window. Let's have some air."

"No, close it up. We'll have smuts in."

Foreign territory. Kidsgrove, Crewe, Chester....

"Sit down! Shut up! I can't wait to see the sea!"

And after an interminable while: "It's there! The sea! I can see the boats!"

We clanked into Rhyl station and walked into town, where we were briefed and left to our own devices. After the obligatory purchase of a decorated tin bucket and spade, my brother caught sight of an enclosure within which a score of cyclists were racing on a variety of knock-about machines. The bucket and spade hastily relegated to second place, we paid our pence and joined the melee on a pair of brakeless trikes. Round and round the track we sped until the attendant called Time.

Then to the sands. Until the early Fifties, concrete anti-tank pyramids lined the beaches at Rhyl and other resorts. These had been hastily laid down shortly before the war and now served variously as castles, jumping towers, climbing frames and Places to Graze Yourself On. My brother and I managed to perform all these feats before he got lost and my father had to pay a visit to the Lost Children Stand. My brother turned up none the worse for wear half an hour later, accompanied by a woman who had "found him wandering."

We marched back to the station, tired and triumphant, clutching our Rhyl rock, a pair of snow-storm paperweights and memories of walking along the promenade in our underpants because my mother had forgotten to pack our swimming trunks.

We found our compartment and settled songless into the plush seats. The Club Trip was over for another year, leaving us tired, happy and, if provoked, irritable. We reached Crewe in the dusk, and the sleeping train clattered through darkness on to the Loop Line.

"Wake up, Bill. Come on Michael. Time to get off."

We dispersed with brief "goodnights" and the half-conscious plod of tired feet up the homeward road.

End of war celebrations in Lime Street, Tunstall. Grandma Ridgway hangs onto me and cousin Pat as my Mum looks on.

11. I'LL GET THE MANAGER TO THROW YOU OUT

When the mood took us, my friends and I would eschew the cinemas of Hanley and Tunstall for the Smallthorne bug hut. Famed for its audience participation, this survival from the age of silent movies was tucked inconspicuously into a street of terraced houses.

For a modest charge you entered a minute auditorium thick with fug and pin-pricked by a galaxy of glowing Park Drives. It exuded a neighbourly intimacy. The regulars, not only local miners, potters and teenagers, but some from far-flung Tunstall and Sneyd Green, considered the place a second home.

Loud greetings were exchanged with latecomers and usherette alike. Exhortations to keep quiet added to the mayhem. Rory Calhoun struggled against a tide of sweet wrappers, crisp bags and oaths which threatened to engulf him. No matter how hot the romance, how violent the punch-up, how forceful the dialogue, how curvaceous the woman, he and his like were irrelevant to the real business of the evening.

"'ello, Alf. Ah see tha's come without tha lady."

"'er's 'avin' one off."

"'er's alwees 'avin' one off. Canna thee afford bring 'er?"

"Shurrup. We're tryin' watch the film down 'ere."

"'ey dunna understand it, duck."

"Sit down over there or I'll ask the manager to throw you out."

"'ear that, Alf? Yer'll be out in th' gutter with tha whippet."

The design of the Queen's left a lot to be desired. To avoid the projector beam, those in the top seats had to assume a permanent crouch since it passed only inches above the heads of even the shortest patrons. Full use was made of this facility by those who sought a more active participation in the film. At a moment's notice they could throw a variety of gigantic animals across Rory's face using only their fingers and an occasional profile. From time to time the number of fingers used was reduced to two.

"That's a rabbit."

"Dunna talk soft. It's a' antelope."

"Pack it in. Tell 'im, Doris."

"I'm not tellin' you lot again. Pack it in or I'll ask the manager to throw you out."

"'e couldn't throw confetti at a weddin'."

"Throw 'em out theesen, Doris."

"And you can shut up, too."

Doris - I can't remember the usherette's real name - seemed to pass entire evenings scurrying from one hot-spot to the next. Like a torch-wielding member of the United Nations, she endeavoured to rout trouble the moment it began. But the mob was laying traps. An entire row oscillated like a swing boat, propelled by 20 pairs of feet in unison. Doris rushed to the scene. The row stilled abruptly, its incumbents drawing intently on their fags and gazing with innocent rapture at the screen. After fixing their lit faces with a glare of admonition, she departed to the rear. Her back turned, the rockers rocked anew. This time they were joined by other rows, giving the impression the entire cinema was afloat on stormy seas.

"That's it. I'm bringin' 'im down," stormed Doris.

"I'm coming to get you, Ramini," declared Rory.

"Shut up and keep quiet. It's cost me a day down the pit to see this film." (A voice from the beam)

"I bet they ca'stna' make a camel." (A shout from below)

"Hey, duck, save us your lollipop stick. I'm makin' a model yacht." (Somebody's chat-up line)

And so it went on throughout the 1950s. The Queen's was the only local cinema where the entertainment was provided by the audience rather than the film. To enter was to step back in time even then. Rory Calhoun, Ava Gardener, Gregory Peck and Marilyn played incongruously to a hall which would have been more receptive to the likes of Chaplin, Buster Keaton and the Keystone Cops.

At the time of writing it's still miraculously intact. I wonder where they are now, those seat shakers, saboteurs and amateur comedians? Probably wired into the Net, reformed non-smokers to a one. And I expect Doris handed in her torch long ago. Isn't that so, Doris?

"Shut up or I'll get the manager to throw you out."

Another VE street celebration in Stoke.

'A glimpse of Potteries' life': Etruria in the early 1950s.

MORE PLACES

The places I visited in my youth were the warp and weft of my everyday life and are etched on my mind as vignettes undimmed by the passing years. Chatterley Whitfield Colliery, Knypersley Lake, Hanley Market, the Victoria Hall, Trentham Gardens, and even 1960s London are both the disparate threads of a rag-bag of recollections and the unifying fabric of a past era..

Chapters

1. The Clank of the Pit Tubs (Sept 1999)

2. Lords of our Domain (July 1999)

3. Trouble in the Fo'c'sle (Feb 2003)

4. Done up in Your Best (Feb 1999)

5. Me, Mozart & The Count (Nov 2001)

6. The Beautiful People (Aug 2002)

7. Stellar City (Sept 2002)

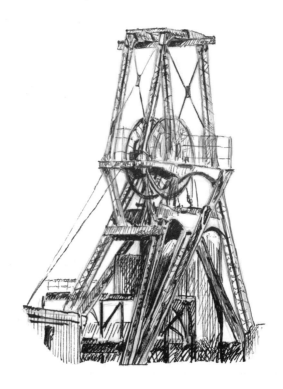

1. THE CLANK OF THE PIT TUBS

The pit lay almost on the doorstep of our new home. From our front garden, two features pierced the eastern skyline - the chimney and spoil heap of Chatterley Whitfield Colliery. Though the colliery has long since ceased to function, the towering stack and the sprawl of industrial buildings remain. The waste tip, once one of the highest in Europe, was contoured and seeded more than twenty years ago. It serves as a stark reminder of the days when the mine was producing thousands of tons a year, and of the lives spent and sometimes given in the quest for coal.

The quickest way to reach Knypersley Lake from our house was via the colliery. The lake was a frequent Saturday venue, but we spent as long on our stop-start journey through the complex as by the waterside. It probably wasn't open-house, but it seemed like it. As a boy of 14 I felt free to wander wherever the mood took me. I traversed the coal sidings at will, lingered by Polly or Phoenix, hissing steam in readiness for the climb to Chell, and listened to the clank of a cage or the whir of its cable as it spun between winding house and pit.

I took a visual inventory of the buildings. They seemed to be at once united and disparate. Gimcrack sheds stood alongside Victorian structures. A latticework of pipes and girders abutted gaunt buildings whose vast open doors revealed couplings, chains and wagon wheels amid the detritus of repair. Rainbows arched across a slat-sided tower through which water showers coursed. And the cavernous mouth of Hesketh Pit yawned from the lane side, at intervals disgorging its cargo of coal and colliers into the sunlight.

Across a wide expanse of patchy asphalt stood a more recent addition to the range of buildings. It housed a shower block on which notices prohibiting smoking were stuck for the benefit of indigenous miners as well as the small number of expatriate Italians who had found employment at Whitfield after the War. Niente Fumare. No smoking. I'm not sure the grammar was right, but these were the first Italian words I knew. Perhaps they were responsible for my Italian O-level success a couple of years later. I don't know. At any rate, I've never smoked since.

Whitfield Road linked Biddulph Road to Cornhill. That it must once have been a narrow, hedge-lined track is evidenced by the handful of farm buildings which it serves to this day. When coal was found, the road lost much of its identity. Its pre-colliery status was abruptly curtailed by the encroaching structures which made its hedgerows redundant, shot pipe-lines over its head and poured slurry into the ditches. The tip grew higher by the day. It reminded me of the pictures I'd seen as a child of the Great Pyramid. The tracked bucket fascinated me. I followed its upward path, the counter-weight to the spoil-loaded hopper simultaneously descending, until it reached the summit and noisily discharged another cargo.

Banky Brook, which ran beneath the spoil, had long since been culverted. It emerged beyond the waste as a turgid steam which nevertheless supported shoals of minnows. We assisted their escape from a contaminated death by imprisoning them in jam-jars and bearing them home like oblations to the gods. A decade before, the risk of bombing had made shelters necessary. They were of the kind of war-time concrete which seemed capable of withstanding a nuclear blast, and were situated off Whitfield Road to the south of the colliery. Camouflaged under a grass canopy, they provided us with the working-class equivalent to Enid Blyton's smugglers' caves. The Famous Five had their torches, and so did we; they explored mysterious passages, the scene of nefarious deeds. The only nefarious deeds we got up to was the occasional drag on a shared butt, but the dark interior of the shelter was certainly explored and mysterious.

A camaraderie existed among the miners we met, though a hierarchy was evident in the revered tones reserved for the 'Face Men'. I caught the general adulation. These miners at the face were no ordinary mortals. Not for them the engineering shop or the lamp house. These men were the glamorous elite of the industry, willing to forsake the daylight for the greater glory of winning the black stuff from the ground. And they had a well paid job for life - at least, until the mine shut down. But the planned disintegration had set in long before. My father-in-law, Fred Warburton, who had begun in the winding house at 13 and continued there for the next 40 years, went with the rest. The reserve of coal remained where it was first laid down, the mineral line was made into a Greenway, the tunnel was filled in, the spoil-heap landscaped and the ghosts of those who had given their strength and breath in daily toil were laid to rest.

Yet at odd times, when I've visited the site since, I can swear I've heard the clank of pit tubs leaving the shaft and the whisper of the cable cutting the air.

2. LORDS OF OUR DOMAIN

Knypersley Lake in the 1950s was the favourite weekend haunt of young colliers and others living on the edge of the city. It was a mile from the nearest bus-stop, but most walked. We took a short cut through Chatterley Whitfield Colliery. A path led to the hamlet of Ridgway, hence down to the Trent Valley on which the reservoir lies. The valley remains unspoilt, a gem close to the sprawl of suburbs.

The reservoir was built in the 1860s to feed the Trent and Mersey Canal. It represented a triumph of civil engineering in its day, and though its gritstone overflow might be seen as obtrusive by some, I always felt it presented a benign face to the mill pond which lay below it in the valley. Elements of the landscape as it was before the reservoir was completed remain. The mill at the foot of the overflow is unchanged and was once used, I think, as a Scout hut.

The route of the original lane can be partly traced where it deviates from the dam road at the foot of the hill leading to Bemersley. The heavily wooded valley, filled by the embryo Trent, was transformed into a picturesque leisure retreat for the local mining plutocracy. Owned in turn by Hugh Henshall Williamson, James Bateman and Robert Heath, by the 1950s it was in the hands of the water board, who kindly allowed the masses, of which I was one, free rein.

A previous owner, who had money to burn, had erected a folly known as the Warder's Tower in the Puginesque style of Victorian fantasy. In the mid 1950s it was occupied. By whom I don't know, but it must have been a welcoming abode since whenever I cast a look in its direction smoke from its ornate chimneys was inevitably wreathing above the trees.

A bridge had been contructed across the Trent stream as it entered the lake. The bridge's graceful arch complemented the tower, and boat rings, still miraculously in place, had been leaded into the masonary probably at Williamson's or Heath's request. The water at that point is deep, and those men who had been watching Johnny Weismuller's Tarzan often took the plunge from a ledge which ran below the parapet to the feigned adulation of their girl-friends. The divers hit the water 20 feet below. From the bridge you could make out their etiolated bodies as they sank and rose to the surface in a sleek parabola.

We never tired of exploring. Unimpressed by the history of the place, we thrashed a path to Lion's Paw Wood using sticks as machetes, tried unsuccessfully to contact the Spirit of Gawton's Well and tracked the boulder-strewn Trent towards its source. The area was littered with reminders of its past. A ruined boat-house stood at the far end of the lake. Here and there mysterious half-buried walls rose through marsh and marsh-marigold. Dressed-stone bridges spanned a maze of overgrown feeders and a steeply-sloping path tunnelled through shale cliffs - a further testament to the caprice of our wealthy forbears.

I must have been 14 when I first came across the Serpentine. Before then, I had never ventured to the far side of the Big Lake. Some self-imposed restriction had rendered it off-limits, and the focus of our activities had been the Warder's Tower. But for some reason we found ourselves pushing along a path we had never used before and emerging on an earth dam overgrown with shrubs and trees. Through a gap between trunks I made out a brackish pool winding below an untrod region of dense woodland - the Serpentine. Until then I had a preconception of Knypersley Lake in much the same way the Early Church viewed the Earth's position in the planetary hierarchy. I thought I knew its boundaries and I was surprised to discover I didn't. I was Carter, and the tree-reflecting water below me was Tutankhamun's tomb, waiting to be explored. And we did. We were the only ones there, apart from a woman who appeared from nowhere to tell us "You shouldn't be here. I'll tell Mr Heath when I get in." At the time, the last of the Heaths still lived alone at Greenway Bank Hall, a local gem gratuitously demolished by the Biddulph Council in the 1970s. The woman must have worked there.

Throughout the summers of 1954 and 1955 the Serpentine was home to us. We roasted inedible potatoes over wood fires by the lake side, swam through verdigris shallows into the clear reaches and sought ways amid the overgrown paths. No one ever disturbed us. We were the lords of our domain, abroad in strange lands - not more than two miles from Chatterley Whitfield's clanging cage.

It's still there. Councilised, accessible, dogwalked, mapped and funded, but there. And a thousand miles from the charred potatoes we ate at dusk 50 years ago.

3. TROUBLE IN THE FO'C'SLE

According to Kenneth Graham, "there is nothing, absolutely nothing, half so much worth doing as simply messing about in boats." I must say I agree. However, apart from an occasional leisurely row around Tunstall Park lake, I had little chance to practice my oarsmanship. Then one Sunday I ventured to Knypersley with two companions and put my skills to the test. Lying on the bank near the present car park was the remains of a dead tree. It was of considerable weight, but with patience and effort we managed to get it into the water.

We must have gone equipped for a swim, for we had bathing trunks to hand. Finding the tree trunk was one of those serendipities that occur throughout one's boyhood. Leaving our clothes under a convenient bush, we pushed the tree into the shallows and clambered aboard. Our first attempts to manoeuvre it were doomed to failure. Three pairs of hands provided insignificant propulsion for so large a vessel and we resorted to legs instead. While I, the navigator, straddled the tree, my companions eased themselves overboard and proceeded to generate sufficient speed to take it to the other side.

The peaty water was bitterly cold and of an incalculable depth; nevertheless we struggled on until we had reached the halfway mark. When our ship had gathered sufficient momentum to take it in the direction of the opposite bank, the other two joined me in the fo'c'sle with such energy that the tree spun around, tipping the three of us into the murky depths. We clambered aboard with difficulty, but now the previously submerged part of the tree lay uppermost. And it was crawling with beetles. Every size and variety was represented. I had no idea until then that beetles were able to survive a quick dip. Perhaps the specimens now exploring my legs were an amphibious genus unknown to all but the most obsessive collector. The depth of water precluded any notion of leaving the tree and swimming to shore, so we had to put up with the extra passengers.

We managed to blank out the horror of it all until we touched ground, at which point we made a rapid departure, flicking the remaining insects from our legs as we went. The only problem was how to get back to the other side. It was too far to risk a swim, and we would feel pretty conspicuous making the half mile journey up the lane dressed only in trunks. I think we settled for

another boat trip. But only after turning the tree to its former position in the
hope that our unbidden guests would suffer slow death by drowning. It hadn't
worked before, but it might if they were under for long enough. We put to
ground where we had started out. As we reached the bank I trod on some
sharp underwater object which necessitated a visit to hospital and four
stitches. Apart from that everything went to plan.

The next time I visited the lake it was with a limp and a resolve to leave
aquatics to the baths. I decided to take the path which led by the Warder's
Tower into unexplored territory. At the time, the mid-50s, the tower was still
inhabited. I don't know who lived there, although various rumours circulated.
One had it that it was a gamekeeper's house, another that gypsies had made
their home there. I can vouch for neither, since all I ever saw was an occasional
plume of smoke rising behind the trees. It wasn't long before the tower was
deserted, the open door a tempting diversion for a nosy person like me with
time on his hands. I climbed the winding stairs to the top, passing through three
or four rooms in the process. There wasn't much to do once aloft, but for a
moment you were monarch of all you surveyed.

The tower, with its heraldic badge, was a place of Arthurian mystery.
The atmosphere was intensified by Gawton's Well, a little further along the
track. Here an ancient spring trickled through basins and conduits of worked
stone. A carpet of pine needles hushed the site, itself bounded by a
rectangular wall and overhung with brooding trees. The quiet here seemed
palpable and the slight breeze bore the breath
of Merlin. At least that's what I used to think as
I left the spot, my pace quickening with every step.

These places have retained their poignancy
over the years. The lake, with its vast open space of
grey water; the tower, with its Rapunzel
associations; and Gawton's Well, from which
unseen eyes gaze forever out.

4. DONE UP IN YOUR BEST

Wherever you lived in the Potteries, Hanley was the place to visit. Until the late Fifties you wore your best for the expedition and travelled there by bus or Loop Line train.

The Chell bus dropped you off outside Marks and Spencer's. The railway station was in a cutting adjacent to the Grand Hotel. You could get to Hanley quicker by bus or train than nowadays by car. High Lane was empty of all but the odd tradesman's van, and cars were few enough to afford PMT, Rowbotham's and Stonier's a straight-through route with only short stops to pick up passengers. You could set your watch by the trains. The station was nearer the town centre than many of the present-day car parks. There was no road-rage because the factors which precipitate it were absent; travelling in was part of the fun, part of the day. Service was practically door to door.

Everyone who went to Hanley visited the Market. It remained at that time a proud testament to the Victorian vernacular. Its soot-blackened masonry formed the northern wall of the square and was embellished by a line of fluted urns. Sherwin's occupied a corner position and sold sheet music and instruments. If I had money for a vanilla slice I went next door to the cake shop, where smocked girls presided over the fancies and called customers by their first name.

The main entrance to the Market was protected by a pair of heavy gates which were swung against the wall on shopping days. The market's sounds and smells were unique and carried through the cavernous interior into the square. The building had never been part of the 20th century. That was its charm - and a reason for its demolition. It was locked into a Dickensian time warp even then, reluctant to escape, patronised by the hordes of customers who savoured its anachronism.

The market was frugal and welcoming. Stalls lined the slabs, pigeons cooed from the cast-iron roof and a translucent light filtered through panes grimy with years. The whole place echoed: to puppies in the pet gallery, exuberant sellers, the voices of the crowd, the scuffle of crates across the stones, the muted footsteps of people in the square. And mingled with the sounds, the smell of cabbages and crowds, red lead and vented air.

An arcade ran alongside Lewis's. It had a mosaic passage serving a number of well-used shops and was bent halfway down its length, like a knuckle of pork. I remember the arcade photographer's. Whenever I went to Hanley I always hovered for a moment outside this shop. It invariably displayed a sheet of black and white prints showing the same face in perhaps 40 poses. I suppose one selected the most flattering and ordered an enlargement. It seemed an eminently sensible way to do business and must have given the customers an opportunity to escape the small, crinkle-edged snaps which were about all their Brownie could manage.

On the rise of the square stood what used to be the Angel Hotel. It was an imposing building which has now been whittled to a fifth of its former size but whose vaults are still used as a pub. On the same side, almost opposite the shamefully derelict St John's Church, stood a chapel which had been converted into a skating rink. My inauguration into the pastime began there. Sometimes I made the journey to Hanley simply to enjoy the chance of colliding with the barrier or of displaying my skills to the few more amateur than myself.

On occasions my luck would be out and there were no skates to fit me. (I took size 11 even as a young teenager). The girl would cast a disdainful look in my direction and I came to believe my feet had entered into a conspiracy against her employers. But eventually a regulation pair would turn up and I was off for an hour around the shiny grey concrete in the company of veterans, novices and those to whom St John's - not the church - beckoned.

The remnants of a football ground lay behind St John's Church. The area now forms part of the Potteries Shopping Centre. Long disused even in the Fifties, it stood abandoned and forlorn amid blown newsprint and clip-top bottles until land prices rose sufficiently to make its acquisition viable. The place had a ghostly feel to it. The shattered terraces were plainly visible, with here and there a defiant trace of some once important structure poking through the debris. It was quite accessible and used as a short cut to reach Town Road from the back of the market.

I supposed the last remnant of post-war Hanley was Bratt and Dyke's. Now that, too, has succumbed, although the building remains intact and has in some indefinable way retained an echo of its former status. I visited it often, with my mother, then my wife. It had an *Are You Being Served?* feel, and although I remember no blue-rinse ladies overseeing pattern-hunting housewives, I am sure Mrs Slokum would have been more than willing to lend a hand.

Successive councils saw Hanley as the city centre, the way forward. They have never really succeeded, partly because of the geography of the city, partly because of the strong identity of individual townships, each with its parochial tradition. Yet it remains a centre of sorts.

The facade of the market at least could have been spared. It was shored up instead, said to be "unstable". Really? The Potteries Shopping Centre might be glitsy, warm and cheerful. Unfortunately you can't buy back your heritage with a truck load of bricks.

'A gateway to freedom': Dunwood looking from Endon in the 1950s.

'A cinema in every street':
The crowds flock to see *Psycho* in Hanley, above, and The Picture Palace in Tunstall, below.

5. ME, MOZART ☞ THE COUNT

Everyone knew the Victoria Hall in Hanley. Count Bartelli, the masked demon of the wrestling circuit, was familiar with its floor, Elgar and Paderewski with the podium, and the redoubtable Councillor Boon knew well its acoustics.

I heard Rachmaninov's Second Piano Concerto there. Later, it was The Temperance Seven, and later still, HMS Pinafore. But despite the music Councillor Boon still insisted on putting in an appearance. He turned up at our annual school Speech Day one evening in the 1950s and delivered his encomium to a bemused (and amused) audience after the last awkward strains of a Mozart ensemble had died away.

The music was provided by the school orchestra, a labouring band of would-be musicians who rarely hit the right note and whose contribution to the classical repertoire left much to be desired. The conductor was impressive in his wielding of the baton. Unfortunately his charges found it difficult to respond to this enthusiasm and appeared to the audience to be making solo performances of a variety of pieces. As time wore on, I was alerted to the odd chuckle escaping from a seat close by. In a vain attempt to regain my own composure, I turned my eyes beyond the players to the school staff. They occupied several tiers and looked resplendent in the gowns and ermine which attested to their status as academic giants. Unfortunately, these erudite gentlemen appeared to find the band's offering even more risible than did the audience.

My maths teacher in particular, a stalwart disciplinarian, was losing the battle to control his face. Even as I watched he produced a large handkerchief with which he pretended to wipe his nose. Unable to maintain the deception, he threw caution to the wind and, taking off his spectacles, sobbed into his hands. The sight of his shaking shoulders had little effect on either instrumentalists or conductor. Indeed, now they were into their second wind and blissfully unaware of the contorted faces both to the fore and rear.

Mercifully the end came. The applause which followed had less to do with enthusiasm for Mozart than gratitude for making the evening go with a swing; not quite the swing the conductor had in mind, perhaps, but a swing nevertheless. And into the vacuum stepped Councillor Boon. Perhaps he was as ignorant as the orchestra as to what constituted good music, or maybe he was too wrapped up in his own part in the proceedings to care. His speech was to be the high point of the evening and he intended to deliver it memorably. This was an occasion to be proud of. He knew it. The audience knew it. The band knew they were nothing more than a warm-up act and they sat in silence, fiddling with their bows. "Ladies and gentlemen," he began, turning his Arthur Lowe glasses to the light. "Welcome to another 'anley 'igh skeow Speech Day." I recall his speech took up the next half hour, rapidly mitigating the effects produced on us by the previous act.

At around this time, I took an interest in the wrestling matches which took place at the Victoria Hall on Saturday nights. Apart from Count Bartelli, I've forgotten the names of the other contestants of the time, but the couple of hours I spent watching them were far better value than any speech day. Unaccountably, it isn't the throw-about antics of the wrestlers that stick in my mind, but the audience response. Like an echo of the days of blood-tub theatre, the crowd were able to divide the contestants into good and bad guys the moment they left their changing rooms.

The good guys were the ones who drew the sympathy. The baddies, on the other hand, drew a ferocious opprobrium from onlookers, who lost little opportunity to cast doubts on the baddy's parentage and to berate him for the harm he appeared to be inflicting upon his victim. Indeed, some less restrained members of the audience felt impelled to walk to the ring and offer advice through the ropes. Among their number was a middle-aged Mrs Merton character who, armed with a perpetual umbrella, lost no time in leaping to the ring and lashing out at the object of her fury.

They don't make 'em like that any more. And I'm not talking umbrellas.

6. THE BEAUTIFUL PEOPLE

Trentham Gardens was another popular destination through the 50s and 60s. The two principal attractions were the miniature railway and the wonderful art deco lido, now (predictably) demolished.

A railway branch line built for day trippers terminated opposite the entrance and is an indication of the strength of visitor numbers in pre-war years. I can't remember travelling there by train. I do, however, recall going there by bus, coach, and later by car.

As a child I was both fascinated and puzzled that such a large expanse of water and such a wealth of trees could be found so close to the city. I had become used to the claustrophobia of what is now termed 'the built environment' and I had relegated the real countryside to far-off regions which had nothing to do with our council house nor my grandfather's Tunstall back-to-back. Yet here was Trentham, a veritable wonderland but a stone's throw from the last housing ribbon.

We took a picnic and allowed ourselves an open-necked shirt (always worn over the jacket lapel, never under) if the thermometer climbed past 70F. The minute the last mouthful of cheese had been scoffed it was time for the miniature railway. My brother and I couldn't rest until we had paid the fare, examined the locomotive and climbed on board. A brief hoot signalled departure and off we rumbled.

The lake glinted through the trees, the trees sailed through the clouds, the wheels click-clacked along a track burnished silver and deep in humus. Now we were going. Now we were really thundering along. I was riding the number-plate of the Flying Scotsman. We were doing 80! I caught a glimpse of Dick Barton's trilby poking around a tree trunk. Maybe he was after trout. Or maybe he had been sent to save the train as it sped to derailment along the margins of the lake. No-one seemed to know. No-one cared. There was no-one special on board anyway. Just men in caps, wives holding their plaited daughters and boys swishing wands at the trackside ferns.

Sometimes we didn't do the round trip. We got off at the pool instead. This was about half way along the lake, situated in a bowl cut from rising land. It was Posh with a capital P. Not a Potteries P, but a less parochial version to be found in the sun-kissed Home Counties or in Rupert Bear's

Nutwood. An air of sophistication clung to its white-rendered brickwork. Bathers lounged in clusters about the lawns. They could have stepped from the pages of the National Geographic, such was their gloss- paper appeal.

I mounted the steps and entered an aquatic version of the Tunstall Ritz. Who needed those teeth-glinting portraits of the Hollywood Greats? The really beautiful people were all here. They had come along for a quick dip and douse, and one of them was already displaying himself on the top stage before committing himself to the great plunge.

I was no Johnny Weissmuller, and no doubt he would have scoffed at the height of the diving board which filled me first with awe and later, when I was on it, trepidation. I have no doubt it would have paled into insignificance alongside those in Santa Barbara, but it was certainly high enough for me. Perched aloft with the rooks and feeling conspicuous, three divers had already shown their mettle while I cowered further back, waving nonchalantly to my parents far below to show I was taking it all in my stride. I never risked a dive, kidding myself the rough concrete bottom would abrade my skin. But I did pluck up the courage to jump. It was a long time before I hit the water.

The first of my visits to the pool are lost to antiquity, but must have been in the early 1950s. A decade later I had become one of the beautiful people too, lounging in my shades and Sean Connery shorts and giving the eye to any Ursula Andress who came into range.

The railway no longer exists. When I last visited the gardens, a short length of wall, part of the lido complex, was still visible amid mounds of rubble bulldozed across the site. As for the rest, it seems rather like the ghost of a place I once knew. The main features are instantly recognisable: the lake, the remains of the old hall. I suppose what is missing are the people, beautiful or otherwise. And the click-clack of carriage wheels echoing through the woods en route to divers' paradise.

7. STELLAR CITY

I was a frequent visitor to London throughout the 50s and 60s, sometimes with friends or girlfriends. Later my wife and I drove down or used the Midland Red buses, staying with relations in Harrow. Then, as now, London prices quickly relieved you of any money you might have - so our excursions never lasted longer than a few days.

My mother's family came from Deptford and I was born in Greenwich, so I had strong ties to the City. Even as a lad of 15 my younger brother was entrusted to my care on tube journeys to the South Kensington Museums, where we flitted with delight between dinosaurs and pumping engines. London then was a wonderland, and retained its joie de vivre throughout the following two decades.

The 1960s was its crowning glory, where a palpable excitement rang through the streets and one had the sense of being at the centre of the universe. I recall Leicester Square in the late summer dusk, camera crews perched on ledges to film The Beatles as they stepped from their limousine into a theatre where they were giving a debut concert. Then there was my first risqué visit to Ronnie Scott's Jazz Club, a subfusc warren of loud music, cigarette smoke and sweater-clad silhouettes. And a visit to the Tower to see the Crown Jewels. The fledgling tourist industry made little impact on our enjoyment, and my wife and I spent half an hour scrutinising the treasures alone and in silence.

Driving into London now is not for the faint hearted. In the 1960s there was less traffic at Hyde Park Corner than now at Burslem lights. Parking was no problem. I remember parking my Wolseley behind actor Leslie Phillips' Mercedes as he stepped out and made his way to the theatre. Ironically, we were going to the same play.

It was not unusual to see celebrities in the street. They were just as ignored as the rest of us. A pleasant bustle was the order of the day, not the frenzied hubbub which nowadays accompanies the crowds in Oxford Street and Piccadilly Circus. It was a young, stellar city, at the height of fashion. The girls wore black eyeliner, mini skirts and knee-length boots. Many had elaborate bouffant hairstyles. Men had their hair long and wore open shirts and jeans.

Unlike now, I never had the slightest apprehension of going anywhere at any time. It was a remarkably crime-free city. Drugs were virtually absent. Not only was mugging unknown; the word itself hadn't been invented. It was a wonderfully homogeneous city. The policy of so-called multi-culturalism hadn't been instigated since there was no need to do so.

The Kinks' Waterloo Sunset sums up 1960s London to me more than any other song. Whenever I hear it, my mind conjures up a vivid, almost ethereal image of time and place. The Thames is bathed in the blush of a summer's evening. The sky is a deep sapphire. The bridges are sprinkled with light. The roar of slow-moving traffic is reduced to a hum. Thanks, Ray Davies, for that.

I don't go to London as often as I did. The adrenalin rush is still there, but it's different, vaguely threatening. The pavements are still as hard and distances just as deceptive, but that sunlit 1960s' palette has dulled and the colours have lost their sparkle. It's dirtier than it was, and the vast numbers thronging the streets are leading to social meltdown. The feeling I had of being one with the rest has been lost. Now I'm a stranger re-entering the home where I grew up, but finding everything altered.

The jewel in the crown of English culture will never be the same. I look back and mourn its passing.

WORK & PLAY

My early pursuits lacked the frenzied application which has become a hallmark of life in the 21st century. We took our pastimes seriously - but not too seriously.

There were none of the pressures of work suffered by schoolchildren nowadays, and even as a grammar school lad, expected to do well in exams and all the rest of it, there was time and space to indulge in any hobby which took my fancy. The pace of life was unhurried. It wasn't essential to be a 'team player'. And you were unlikely to need a counsellor if things didn't go according to plan.

I never felt I had to compete with anyone, nor did I feel an onus to achieve the unachievable. What remained was the enjoyment of doing things for the pleasure they gave, and not to meet an arbitrary target set by someone with a check list. Employment was treated in a similar way. We worked to live rather than the other way around.

I hope the following articles will rekindle those times when life was lived at a slower pace, and where the adage 'more haste less speed' was a guiding principle for many.

Chapters

1. Transport Heaven (Sept 2001)

2. Marbles or Rinkers (Feb 2002)

3. Back on the Tiles (July 2001)

4. Flying Through the Nets (July 2002)

5. Jimmy Murphy is Dead (April 2000)

6. A Missing Digit (March 2001)

7. Two Conventional Hands (April 2001)

8. For the Price of a Licence (Aug 2001)

9. All Marvellous Stuff (March 2002)

10. Steaming Terylene (Nov 2002)

11. The Sans-Culotte (Oct 2000)

12. Bow Legs & Knock Knees (March 2003)

1. TRANSPORT HEAVEN

My parents must have bought me the lorry for Christmas. It came from a shop in Tunstall Square, near the Home and Colonial. For some time the lorry reigned supreme in my toy cupboard. It was a scale model, clockwork driven and rubber-tyred, and by turning a crank I could raise the back to disgorge a cargo of crayons, blocks or anything else that came to hand. The lorry was constructed of steel plates held together with tiny brass bolts, and it shone a glossy green under the living room light. A couple of spanners had been provided with which to disassemble or rebuild the entire vehicle should the mood take me. It was the sort of toy beloved of those with an eye to a future in haulage.

Its substantial weight added to its attraction. Such was its prestige, it was carefully garaged in its cardboard box each night and no one but myself was permitted to take it out. Friends were allowed a covetous look on the understanding they kept their fingers to themselves and didn't try to wind it up while my back was turned.

Its clockwork innards were disguised by the body and only the truly vigilant were able to point out the huge main spring tucked away beneath the cab window. I dreamt of being able to wind the spring to its full potential and release the lorry at full speed in the empty school hall. I could imagine it racing across the polished parquet, its miniature steering wheel set to take the vehicle spiralling into transport heaven. As it happened, I never got the chance to do this and my lorry was consigned to oblivion at a much later date.

I seemed to have a penchant for a wide range of wheeled playthings. Well before the lorry, I had acquired a papier mâché Pluto with cord attached. This monstrous toy was the result of a painting competition I had entered at my mother's behest. This involved submitting a version of a Disney character to a prescribed size. The winners would receive a variety of gifts, one of which turned out to be my ghastly yellow dog. A perfunctory knock announced its arrival, and the cardboard box which contained it was manhandled from one of those three-wheeled railway trucks and into our hall. Pluto was extricated without ceremony and hauled around the living room for a few days until the novelty wore off. I am not sure where he ended up, but he was soon to depart my life for pastures new, and I welcomed the respite.

Much more to my taste were my die-cast models of cars. There were Morrises and Wolseleys, Hillmans and Sunbeams, the Morgan three-wheeler and a black Riley. Most were push-along models, but one, like the lorry, was clockwork-driven. It was a Morris 8 series E and its claim to status lay in its ultra-modern built-in headlights. At a time when other cars could only boast headlights on stalks, these new headlights represented a daring departure from tradition. It was given to me by Frank Danby, a shopkeeper in Tunstall High Street and a friend of my father. Getting something for nothing was a novelty to me. I cherished the car for many weeks, taking care not to over-wind it and making sure its paint-work remained unscathed.

Unfortunately, the car and I were unable to withstand the forces of fate. Walking through Tunstall Park one day in the late 1940s, I felt the comforting bulge of the Morris 8 in my jacket pocket and decided to give the car a run there and then. I was standing at the bandstand end of the big lake at the time, near an overflow which fed the smaller boating lake via an underground pipe. I wound the car and released it on the smooth Tarmac. It travelled for some distance without mishap before veering unexpectedly into the water. It plunged down the overflow and disappeared en route to the small lake, a destination it never appeared to reach.

I felt its loss greatly, particularly since it occupied the higher clockwork status and had been given to me as a present. How would I ever be able to stare at Frank's clanging till again without being reminded of gross negligence? In the event I took refuge in my train set. At least that was not destined for the overflow.

2. MARBLES OR RINKERS

Children have forgotten how to play. Nowadays, 'play' has more to do with the cynical manipulation of big business, which launches 'fun' products onto the children's market at prescribed intervals, than to simple pleasures. Transformers, Ninja Turtles, Pokemon were examples. The trick is to nag the hapless parent to buy, while ostracising the child who can't give Pikachu's tail whip rating.

It was not always thus. I had a bag of marbles which I frequently took to Chell School in the late 1940s. The bag was of strong cloth fastened with a drawstring. It contained a variety of treasures, some of glass, others of silvered steel and a few much-prized china examples. My marbles were part of a hierarchy based on size, material, colour or survival rate. Some acquired a legendary significance. The small butterfly-blue of bubbled glass looked commonplace amid its larger and more flamboyant companions. Yet this inconspicuous globe possessed a charmed inner-life and was the survivor of many battles. Whenever I aimed it, it would batten onto its target with the assurance of a heat-seeking missile. The bag's bulging cargo of wins were proof of its magic.

Unfortunately, whatever spell produced its score rate, it wasn't enough to keep it out of the school drain. It was no consolation to know that the drain, unaccountably the centrepiece of many a tournament, was already home to a vast tally of other boys' marbles. Now my Second-in-Command, a medium-sized chromium plated ball, became Commander-in-Chief. There was some dispute over terminology. Whereas I referred to my *marbles*, to others they were shotties, glassies, allies and rinkers - unlike horse chestnuts, which were known universally as conkers. Once the conker season was in full swing my marbles were relegated to a bedroom drawer and the drawstring bag replenished with my new weapons of war.

I remember two games of marbles we used to play. One involved setting four or five in a ring and attempting to 'shoot' them using your own marble; the other was a two-marble game which involved you and a companion aiming alternately at each other's marble, and pocketing the same if you hit it.

Equal precision was necessary if you were to strike a rival's conker a mortal blow. Folk-lore abounded. The best cords came from old football boots. The best conkers had to be pickled in vinegar. That made them hard, and, by extension their owner too. Combat was ruthless, and crowds gathered to watch a particularly interesting contest.

The aim was to smash your opponent's conker to bits while keeping your own intact. Like a prize marble, you had your favourite conker, a revered specimen which had uncannily retained its shape amid many skirmishes.

The element of surrogate warfare which is the basis of all games was also present in Rally-O. Two playtime teams were formed. It was the job of one team to rescue one of its number from a den while the other team tried to prevent this. You considered yourself rescued when touched by one of your team. If one of your team's defenders was also touched by the opposition, he would end up in the den alongside you. I say 'he' since I cannot recall any girl taking part.

You would find the girls skipping elsewhere in the playground. There was no Blairite policy then which would have insisted they threw their ropes away on the grounds of gender discrimination and join the boys in their dens, so they were free to enjoy themselves. Their play had a mystique of its own, and we boys never thought of trespassing upon it. Solitary skippers would chant rhymes to themselves, jogging or hopping through the rope. In more democratic versions, a longer rope would be turned by two girls while a third - or fourth - skipped through it.

I hear the rope's unremitting rhythm as it strikes the asphalt. July's cirrus wisp an otherwise cloudless sky. The boys' voices announce another rescue. From the green strip which runs the length of the playground there comes the soft plock of a cricket ball against a makeshift bat. A shrill whistle-blast marks the end of another break and the cricketers, skippers and rescuers freeze to attention before making their way inside.

If today's toy manufacturers could bottle Rally-O and sell it at so much a litre, there would be dens in the playground even now.

3. BACK ON THE TILES

When I wasn't playing, I was reading comics. That's where Cynthia Pritchard comes in. She would make her way to our house on many a dusky November night. Armed with her Beanos and Dandys, she would give a rent-collector's knock before releasing her cargo on the hall floor. Perhaps 'releasing' is the wrong word, since it implies a certain carelessness. Cynthia was anything but careless, and treated her comics with a reverence at odds with their well-thumbed appearance.

I would disappear upstairs to make my own rapid compilation. I had an entire cache of comics I had read, re-read and at some point thought worthy of discarding. These I would also introduce to the proceedings and there, under a 40-watt bulb, the business of the night would take place. We would begin with the conventions of preamble, exchanging brief, unmeant pleasantries with the glitter-eyed cunning of merchants in some Baghdad bazaar.

First we arranged our comics so that odd titles were enticingly visible to the other party. This was done in silence, with neither of our bundles permitted to touch and, for the time being, ownership retained. But by degrees both swapper's and swappee's fingers fluttered towards the opposition's pile. By tacit consent a page was raised and examined upside down. Should it prove sufficiently inviting, the comic was swivelled tentatively to afford a better view. During these manoeuvres few words were exchanged. A state of feverish anticipation was engendered, and the laying on of hands became increasingly audacious.

It was usually Cynthia who made the first direct assault on my pile. Her outstretched fingers would descend unerringly on the least battered of my offerings and before I could reciprocate she had added it to her stock. To show she was a fair-minded girl at heart she now traded one of her own comics to complete the transaction. This usually turned out to be a shoddy version of one I had read several times, and which would inevitably come to light on my side of the floor anyway.

But all was not lost. Now the ice was broken, a general scrummage was in order. This was punctuated by quiet intervals in which we each perused a particularly interesting item, tilting the page to savour the artwork under the weak light.

The Bash Street Kids leered at me from ink-splattered desks, while Desperate Dan was contending with a cow pie the size of an aircraft hangar. Lord Snooty, Julius Sneezer, Korky the Cat, Minnie the Minx, Denis and his ambitiously-toothed mongrel, Gnasher, were all appraised for the fun line, the quirkish mannerism and the four-word quip which would enliven many a dull moment in the week ahead.

Cynthia rarely left disappointed. The newly-acquired, previously unread comics safely stowed under her arm, she exited into the night leaving me to count my losses. She had that rare ability to leave with more than she had brought with her. If this gift did not desert her in later life, I am sure she must have gained a foothold near the top of some corporate pole, trading shares to equally hapless victims of her wiles.

Still, I did have my *Eagle* collection. She wasn't going to get her hands so easily on that. *The Eagle* came out some time in the 1950s, and represented a dramatic departure from the world of Desperate Dan and his appetite. Gone the zany adventurers who had been DC Thomson's hallmark since before the war. The new arrivals were altogether a more glamorous lot. My favourite was an intergalactic flyer, the ultra-English Dan Dare who, with his partner Digby, harked back to the Edwardian age of noble heroism.

It was left to Dan to forgo the never-never backstreets beloved of Minnie, Korky and the rest in favour of a quick trip around the Solar System in pursuit of the Mekon, a shady character with a head the size of the Millenium dome. Moreover, *The Eagle* was alluringly packaged in an ample, landscape format whose centre-spread featured a weekly schematic drawing of something like a tank by one Ashwell Wood. No, Cynthia didn't get her grubby little hands on them. But my mother did. I don't know when, but I came to look through past numbers of my favourite comic one day and the entire collection had 'disappeared'. It probably happened during one of those manic spring clean-ups which seem to inflict themselves on mothers at that time of year.

I occasionally come across a battered copy of some 1950s comic lying unbought among the bric-a-brac. I don't make the purchase. I've learned to live without 'Dans' of any description. Yet a glimpse of Korky disporting himself - or herself, I suppose - across the sheet and I'm back on the tiles under an unshaded lamp. And Cynthia's just begun to gloat. Always a bad sign.

4. FLYING THROUGH THE NETS

The advantage of comics was that you could pick up the story without understanding the words. I can't remember the exact time I began to read. I suppose it was at St Mary's Infants' School in Tunstall, but it may have been later, at Chell Juniors. At Chell we called the teacher 'Polly Rubberneck' on account of his, well, unusually long neck. Whatever his physical peculiarities, he encouraged me to enter the magical world of print.

Books can fascinate at any age. When one is very young, and the line between fact and fantasy blurred, they are all the more captivating. I held the laundry basket for Milly Molly Mandy. I took my place beside Noddy as he sped through Toytown. I gripped the wishing chair as it rose through the school roof. Soon I could look down on Chell Cricket Ground as I sailed to my appointment at the wizard's lair, help the witch fill her cauldron or join the pixies in a frolic around the dell. I was an eighth dwarf, a prince and several woodcutters. I knew what I would do to the witch if she tried to shut me in an oven - I would cosh her with the woodcutter's axe. Wicked stepmothers bounded through my waking dreams, forests brooded over solitary travellers, golden geese laid golden eggs and a magic mill made the seas salty.

The Beacon Readers were peopled with head-scarfed Russian women who worked in the land of ogres, cutting hay. A fox tricked the Gingerbread Man and Brer Rabbit tricked the Tar Baby. Palaces sprang from briars and, armed only with a chipped ruler, I hacked my way to the princess.

I eagerly awaited my Rupert Bear Annual every Christmas. My young mind was entranced by Rupert's adventures. It never struck me as odd that a scarfed bear could speak, nor that his father smoked a pipe and wore plus-fours. Rupert's friends were my friends, frequent visitors to my bedside until the Sandman called.

My annuals were treasures of delight. Between the pages I discovered strange robed figures who inhabited underground chambers. Imps sought magic minerals in vertiginous cliffs. Eccentric professors invented eccentric machines. Dragons guarded distant towers. Flying fish skimmed a halcyon sea. Clearly, Nutwood was a very happening place, indefinably Home Counties, vaguely pre-war, a dreamscape of rural England seen through a magic lens.

Then I grew up. My father was the catalyst to my maturing taste, and on my 14th birthday he bought me a copy of Dickens' *Nicholas Nickelby*. I quickly became immersed in the doings of Dotheboy Hall. I raised a fist to Squeers and a hand of sympathy to Smike. I traced the narrative with a critical eye, sizing up pace, tone, colour and characterisation. It was only a story told by a workaholic, but it was a doorway to times and places beyond the backs.

Now I was hooked. I read whatever came to hand. Dickens, Trollope, Austen, Wells, Bennett, Haggard - an endless procession of pensmiths took over my leisure hours. I mourned Nessie's death in *Hatters Castle*, laughed my way downstream in *Three Men in a Boat* and was inwardly grateful when *The Triffids* got their come uppance.

So the foundations were laid for later excursions into a range of fiction, whether it be C P Snow or Frederick Forsyth. In fact, Freddie's ultra-gripping *Day of the Jackal* scores 10 out of 10 for its superb plot. That's not to say I could stomach all that was put in front of me. Virginia Woolf rendered me comatose, Melville's *Moby Dick* lay unfinished on the shelf and I couldn't understand the twelve pages of Joyce's *Ulysses* I managed to get through.

I usually have an ongoing book on the bedside table and there's much still to read. But no matter how clever the novel, is it really so different from the life and times of Rupert Bear? Whatever our age, we still occasionally need to fly through the nets. And a book is much cheaper than a package holiday.

5. JIMMY MURPHY IS DEAD

In a quiet interval during the end of war celebrations I sat fascinated by my grandfather's twist-tapping finger as he prepared to light his pipe. It was a long finger; too slender, I would have thought, to have been of much use to a former collier and bar-room pugilist. He took a Vesta from a box as I anticipated the ritual of lighting and the first blue clouds of exhaled smoke. The match remained unstruck. He rarely spoke, but now, in a rare moment of alacrity, he began to sing:

> *Jimmy Murphy is dead*
> *His troubles are all over*
> *He lies in clover...*

The words were at odds with the sunshine flooding through the window and the rise of laughter from the street-party outside. But I was only five and such incongruities passed me by.

Music, like odour, can evoke snapshot memories with poignant clarity. My musical education continued one summer's day in Miss Martin's class. I was now seven. Our classroom boasted an early Coomber speaker, and it was from this that I first heard a Chopin etude. I had no idea who Chopin was, nor how he had entered so abruptly into the room. I can remember the heat of the day, the French windows thrown open against a cloudless sky and a cascade of notes as the study came to a crashing close.

I was further inaugurated into the Classics by a succession of piano tutors whose musical tastes stopped short of the twentieth century. They would have been appalled at just how catholic my tastes had become. They might have been impressed by my *Für Elise*, but unbeknown to Beethoven or themselves I also kept secret scores of George Shearing and Winifred Atwell. I never told them I spent hours listening to Elvis, Jerry Lee Lewis and Little Richard, who were later to achieve the iconic status formerly reserved for the likes of Mozart and Tchaikowsky. The musical apartheid which existed in the 50s is less apparent now. In any case I never recognised the division of musical styles as representative of the English class structure. As far as I was concerned there were two sorts of music: good and bad.

It's hard to explain the vagaries of the mind. What at the time seemed unimportant can remain with you for life, while upheavals once considered traumatic lie forgotten. And so it is with music. The Everley Brothers' *All I Have to do is Dream* evokes an instant picture of the Macclesfield Street Youth Club I used to attend. I see the table tennis bats poised, a chipped stage, disinterested habitués grouped below the bottle-green dado and hear again the old Dansette churning our their mawkish lyrics.

Then I flick to making soap in the science lab at school, where one member of the class, whose penchant for insubordination was legendary, struck up Lonnie Donnigan's *Rock Island Line* using his boiler tube as air-guitar. The price of his classroom entertainment was three strokes. Lonnie would no doubt have been dismayed that anyone offering so faithful a rendition of his song should fare so badly.

A couple of years later a girlfriend of mine, who had a crush on Frank Sinatra, introduced me to Ol' Blue Eyes and the Nelson Riddle sound. Endless afternoons were spent in the parlour of her Tunstall home (three of us, including Frank) until I'd committed *Witchcraft* and the rest of his *Songs for Swingin' Lovers* to memory. Whenever I hear Sammy Cahn's opening line "Those fingers in my hair..." I'm back in 1959. The motes are rising through the sunlight and her mother's figurines are singing back at me from the polished dresser.

Perhaps the most poignant of memories is evoked by the haunting orchestral strains which preceded Sunday lunch. Again, the smell of roast beef and Jean Metcalf welcoming everyone to another *Two-Way Family Favourites.* "Lance-Corporal Dave Smith who is with the Royal Engineers in Germany is sending all his love to his fiancée Sue in Midlothian. He hopes this record will bring back happy memories of the precious hours they spent together during Dave's last leave. So, Sue, especially for you, here's Donald Peers, *By a Babbling Brook......*" Donald did his best, along with Ronnie Hilton, Madame Butterfly, Bizet's Torreador, Alma Cogan, Bing, The Beverley Sisters, Rachmaninov and others, all under Jean's watchful eye.

As for Jimmy Murphy - the only people aware of his fate seemed to be my family. I've never come across anyone else remotely interested in him. Perhaps my grandfather made him up.

6. A MISSING DIGIT

As a lad I was prey to a succession of odd piano teachers. My mother played piano by ear, and had always been able to knock out a passable *Bye Bye Blackbird* when the occasion presented itself.

In the late Forties and early Fifties piano teachers were rarely out of business. She no doubt wanted me to have the opportunity she had lacked, and learn to "play proper" from a score. I took to the piano as a duck to water. Throughout my life I've gained great pleasure from the instrument, and love to hear it played well. Genre has never been an issue with me; whether it be a Russian maestro playing Rachmaninov, a modern jazz quartet, boogie, rock, blues or honky-tonk, I've always been captivated by the sound.

My father acquired a strange looking instrument to start me off. I now realise that this immense piece of furniture, which in its folded state resembled a kitchen table, was a very early nineteenth century example. The tarnished ivories were chipped throughout the length of the keyboard and I recall it had the beery tone one associates with the accidental spillage of liquor into the works. No one seemed to know where it came from, and my father wasn't saying. I arrived home one day and there it was, occupying most of the living room.

About this time my mother had contacted piano teacher number one. An introductory meeting was arranged and we caught the bus to his home near the Smallthorne roundabout. As a child of eight it had been inculcated in me that it was rude to stare. Yet even at that age I found it perplexing that a tutor who earned his living from teaching the piano should have a finger missing. To my immature mind, two complete sets of digits was a basic prerequisite. Yet from his confident demeanour it seemed this man was either unaware of his shortcoming or safe in the knowledge he could manage perfectly well without the additional encumbrance of a full set.

After a perfunctory greeting, he adjusted the stool and played the first part of a Chopin *Polonaise*. "A promising pupil should reach that standard in five years," he informed us. "I charge two shillings a lesson and I think you'll find that compares well with what others are asking. Books will be extra, and I'll get them for you." I enrolled, and for the next two years presented myself before his polished Broadwood each Wednesday at seven. From him I learned elementary notation and progressed in a more or less linear fashion from single note melodies, containing the odd chord, to simplified classics.

Unfortunately it was not all plain sailing. As time went on, my tutor and his wife became embroiled in a range of domestic disputes. As I waited patiently at the keyboard, I could hear them trading insults of an increasingly vitriolic nature from the next room. These episodes eventually reduced his time with me from the hour I had paid for to less than 30 minutes.

In consequence I bade farewell to my challenged tutor. When I left he was once more on speaking terms with his wife, who brought him endless cups of tea and called him "Darling".

By now, the huge piano my father had brought home mysteriously disappeared, to be replaced by an antiquated organ. Incorporated into this relic was a bellows which were primed by depressing a pair of pedals with alternate feet. The sound thus emitted was of variable pitch and quality and at its worst when pulling out what stops remained. Why the piano was discarded in favour of the organ I was not to know; needless to say, it did nothing for my performance

It soon went, much to the chagrin of our mongrel, who would ululate in time to its distorted cadences. A replacement piano was not long in coming. My father paid £25 for it and it stood in the same place as its enormous predecessor. Largely unmarked and of an acceptable tone, it occupied this niche for several years, during which I would be favoured by the talents of two other members of the piano-teaching profession - each with his fingers intact.

7. TWO CONVENTIONAL HANDS

Shortly after my father acquired our second piano I was put in touch with a new teacher who lived in a large, detached house off Hamil Road, Burslem. I had already covered the rudiments; it would be up to this new man to hone whatever talent I had and to encourage me to attain my full potential. My new teacher could boast two conventional hands, but was predisposed to electric shocks. These were delivered by a dodgy light switch and usually suffered by the musician or his sister.

The small Collard piano occupied a place near the lounge bay across which a pair of heavy purple curtains were drawn. These served not only to keep out the cold, but to deaden the din made by aspiring Paderewskis so that the neighbours would not complain.

My first lesson coincided with a downturn in the fortunes of the wiring system. I arrived in the dark one winter's night and the tutor's sister received what was probably the first shock of the evening when she attempted to switch on the light. Her brother entered at that moment and accused her of undue sensitivity. This brief introduction to the domestic side of his life set the tone for my future visits. I never actually-heard the man perform and for all I knew he would be hard put to play two notes in succession. However, he guided me through increasingly difficult pieces and entered me for various examinations.

Each session lasted an hour, and since I was unable to afford the fare home, I walked. I lived two miles away, and during inclement weather I would run the entire distance with my music stuck up my jumper. This served the twin purpose of keeping the score dry and preparing me for cross country at school the following day.

I ended my excursions into piano with a third tutor who lived not far away from home at Greenbank Road. This retiree from the teaching profession kept a smart house and came highly recommended, according to my father. He was also cheaper, which probably accounted for his popularity. He informed me on our first encounter that I looked "like a ball of marl". I've no doubt he was alluding to my bedraggled appearance, so I pulled up my socks and endeavoured to blend in with my surroundings.

I must have spent a year under his wing. As the time for GCE revision approached, my father reasoned I should put my musical education on hold and concentrate instead on my school studies. This made sense, and I finally abandoned piano lessons shortly after my 15th birthday. In spite of the rigours of GCE and the Sixth Form, however, I still found time to entertain myself and others at the keyboard. My taste became more catholic. Alongside the classical repertoire, I purchased arrangements of popular evergreens by George Shearing, boogies by Winifred Atwell and, long before his work was popularised in film, Scott Joplin rags.

A stint of Saturday work in Tunstall Woolworth's enabled me to indulge my minor talent. Specialising in small instruments and sheet music, a shop in the nearby Haymarket had a good selection of scores in stock and I invariably came away with a playable copy under my arm. At the time an inexpensive series was available for 6d, if you wished to concentrate on the classics. The Lilac edition had no equivalent in popular music, and songs from the shows cost up to twice the amount.

What the Haymarket shop lacked, Sherwin's could usually supply. However, my visits to Hanley were rare and "a treat". Moreover, one had to don one's Sunday garb to go there, such was Hanley's esteem in the eyes of those from Chell and Tunstall. Sherwin's stood more or less where the entrance to The Potteries Shopping Centre is now, and was one of a series of small to medium shops trading from the old market building. One could usefully spend an hour trawling through its shelves for that elusive piece.

Another music shop stood on the corner of Hope Street and offered a similar service. But the real jewel in the crown for a lad of modest means was Hanley library. Here, an entire book of compositions could be loaned for a fortnight. And I didn't have to pay a penny.

8. FOR THE PRICE OF A LICENCE

We switch on the Bush and tune in. A collage of foreign voices gabble down the line before the clipped vowels of Middle England cut through the din. "You are listening to Dick Barton, Special Agent." The band strikes up a rapid, rising sequence of chords underscored by an exhilarating base. We're set for half-an-hour's escape into the world of espionage, Dick's natural element.

As we sit sipping our Dandelion and Burdock, our hands dipping vacantly into the crisp bag, the world through the window lies forgotten and we enter a surreal landscape of arch-villains, daring chases and the triumph of good over - well, the not so good - every six or so episodes. I imagine Dick in trilby and trench mac. I see him as grit-hard but with a sensitive centre, blue-chinned and ageless. He's a treasured guest on our sideboard. He has more adventures in half-an-hour than our ware-packing, pick-wielding estate will boast in a lifetime. I am mesmerised.

Dick is not the only one to treat our hearth as his own. At regular intervals throughout the Fifties, other radio visitors come and go. Billy Cotton's reveille 'Wakey! Wakey!' burst over our roast beef on Sundays, Jean Metcalfe delivered her *Two Way Family Favourites* on Behalf of Loved Ones Serving in Her Majesty's Forces Overseas and Al Read dispelled the grey November rack with his cracks. Then there was Mrs Dale, who kept the world's most compendious diary. Her innocent cut-glass adventures seemed to centre almost exclusively on her husband Jim and were followed with messianic fervour by millions. Listeners couldn't get enough of her slight quotidian adventures and the mini-disasters which were part of her fictional blood-stream. When poor Jim eventually entered that great Sound Studio in the sky, the BBC was inundated with floral tributes.

Another nail-biter was the science fiction series, *A Journey Into Space*. This was Barton without the trilby, transported to strange worlds beyond our ken. And we, too, were willing to be transported from our armchairs for the sake of a tour around the universe.

It is hard to explain to those of a televisual age just how riveting these post-war, shaking banister, shaking sound-track productions were. Props, characters and settings were supplied by the listener's imagination and no doubt each individual had his or her own slant on things. They were a powerful influence in welding the country together, a shared experience which defined us and defied the statisticians' tick-list of what constituted the Structure of Class. Unchallenged by the opportunity for other forms of escape, listeners had time to listen and to reflect. Scripts were intelligent and delivered in an uncompromising BBC accent. Only in our demotic age is this seen as a problem, unacceptably elitist, class-ridden and the rest of the clap-trap trundled out by the cod-psychology department.

The unwelcome truth is that people hugely enjoyed these programmes, laughed with them, cried with them and, whatever their position in the social spectrum, switched on in great numbers to listen to them. For the price of a licence, one had access to the glories of the British literary heritage. *Mrs Dale's Diary* was *EastEnders* without attitude and reflected an age when England was at ease with itself.

Radio also provided a fertile environment for fresh ideas. Unfettered by the nonsense of political correctness, commissioners relied on their gut instincts when it came to choosing new material, and didn't have to defer to some faceless committee whose remit might be at odds with their own. As a result, shows like ITMA gave way to the innovative Goon Show and the like. It became something of a school cult to impersonate Harry Seagoon in his fight against the Yellow Peril, Lo Hing Ding. Eccles, Major Bloodnok and Ernie Splutmuscle were also represented - and rejected by those who loathed this zany show. Yet it entered the entertainment vocabulary of the country and without it television shows like Monty Python could not have existed.

After years in the doldrums, radio is experiencing a renaissance, replacing television worldwide as the main news broadcaster. Television itself has degenerated into a hash of imported quiz shows interspersed with Third Way propaganda. As I reach for the 'off' button, I am reminded of the debt my generation owes to those armchair flights of fantasy enjoyed by the undemeaned masses over 40 years ago, and of the contribution our radio heritage continues to make to our lives.

9. ALL MARVELLOUS STUFF

I have already referred to my father's knack of producing unexpected items whose provenance was a mystery to the rest of us. The first paino arrived that way, later a bellows organ. A lolloping mongrel gained entrance via the same route, and so did our first television set.

The purchase of the television coincided with the Queen's Coronation in1953. The set had a 12 inch tube and a Bakelite cabinet. Reception was mediocre and the picture would roll involuntarily whenever our back was turned. Yet our television was a mark of prestige. None of the neighbours had one, and as a badge of pride my father installed it on a wickerwork table which in turn was hoisted atop a small wooden table almost to ceiling height.

My father was involved in organising Coronation Day festivities for the local children. This included watching television, a rare treat. At least a dozen youngsters spent the afternoon encamped cross-legged before our set, unable to take their eyes off the Queen's coach as it trundled through the drizzle. A cathedral quiet reigned: television was the future, and entitled to respect.

It would be some time before commercial television put in an appearance. Until then, viewers had no choice but to watch the one channel available to them, BBC. And that closed down at 10pm when the national anthem signalled bedtime. The only activity on-screen was a bead of light which faded long after the set had been switched off.

Television continued its fascination for many years after our purchase. At first only my father was allowed to switch it on. We would all sit waiting for the blank tube to 'warm up', a process which took several minutes. I was never quite sure what to make of the opening sequence, which showed a tilting mast from which rings of televisual light spiralled. But it provided a comforting, homely image which heralded the evening's entertainment and it never occurred to anyone to ask why. Neither did we question the intervals between programmes, the not infrequent breakdowns in transmission, the interval bell which rang mid-way through a play and gave you the opportunity to put the kettle on, or the fact newsreaders always spoke with plummy accents and wore evening dress.

During intermissions, programmers made use of what they no doubt hoped were calming influences. Until the next programme was ready to roll

- sometimes literally - we would be presented with dray horses ploughing a furrow, or a pair of hands at the potter's wheel. Complementary music was chosen, jaunty or nostalgic, to accompany the sequences until the announcement was made: "We are now ready to continue with our next programme."

Programmes were, in the main, quintessentially British. Unfettered by the demands of market share, accessibility, Anglo-American 'deals' and political interference, the public service broadcasting available was second to none. I have fond memories of many of those early, idiosyncratic offerings. It was quite possible to live on a council estate and to appreciate Billy Bunter's escapades at Greyfriars, a school indefinably Home Counties and as far removed from our street as you could get. I saw no clash between those wonderful Francis Durbridge thrillers and the local pit mound rising above our neighbours' roof-tops. I couldn't wait to tune in to *Little Red Monkey* or *The Adventures of Tim Frazer*, set in the murdering purlieus of Surrey and Hampshire.

The format of some of the early programmes would be unthinkable today. The Brains Trust, which consisted of four intellectuals debating an issue around a table for half an hour, would be a switch-off. As for A.J.P. Taylor lecturing on the Battle of Waterloo without notes, props or prompts for thirty minutes - forget it. There would be rumbles in Parliament about Best Value and the need to justify the licence fee through broadening the audience base. A.J.P. would be hooked off stage.

Following him would be Muffin the Mule and Andy Pandy. All marvellous stuff, a mirror of a country which knew itself, had pride in its achievements and didn't have to rely on imported ideas to create a show. Now I have a television that's a Rolls-Royce to our first 'Austin 7'. It is remote-controlled, colour, multi-channelled, continuous, worldwide .....and boring. It usually spends its time off. Bring back Tim Frazer and the rest. All is forgiven.

10. STEAMING TERYLENE

By my twenties I watched little television and preferred to be out and about. You may remember I used to frequent the Jazz Club in Burslem. However, the Jazz Club was not the sole beneficiary of my dancing skills. Chief among its rivals was the Crystal Ballroom in Newcastle. I went there for a time on Saturday nights - when my current car was capable of making the trip. Usually it wasn't, so I took advantage of the late bus.

There were usually three of us, occasionally four. Preferred dress at the Jazz Club was made up as we went along and usually consisted of a shapeless sweater and slacks. For the lads, anyway. But a strict dress code was in force at the Crystal and suits were the order of the day. Mine was of terylene and used to steam if I had spent too long on the floor.

The Crystal occupied two floors. The ballroom faced the main entrance and below it was a smaller, more intimate area where dancers could relax behind lattice screens. Whereas the Jazz Club was collegiate, intellectual and seedy, the Crystal was a Mecca of bright lights, revolving globes, regimented fox-trots, bands and bangles.

Groups of bouffant-haired girls protected each other from the predatory attentions of opportunists like myself (although I occasionally struck lucky) while an eight-piece ensemble flew us to the moon and let us play among the stars. The last waltz was Engelbert in slow gear and if you found no-one by then it was time for a solo visit to the late bus. What an indignity that was. The singer, who had seen many a minor drama played out below the rostrum, continued his Sinatraesque warblings as the first of the singles queued for their cloakroom ticket. I remember him as a short, wide-shouldered chanteur with a rich baritone voice. He knew all the standards by heart and sung them to himself, oblivious of the swirlers below who, in more intimate moments, were to be seen mouthing whispered echoes of the lyric in each other's ear.

My third night-spot, and one I attended less frequently than the others, was the Queen's Hall in Burslem. The Queen's was the haunt of Teddy Boys and other questionable characters whose idea of 'being on the floor' was in the prone position. At least, that's how it seemed to me. Like the Crystal, the action wasn't confined to the dance floor; suede-shod customers could be found in substantial numbers propped against the upstairs bar or leaning by a draped concert grand. Meanwhile, down below, Susan Maughan or some equally curvaceous songster continued to serenade the few who were still on their feet.

At rare, prodigal, moments I managed two venues in a single night. I particularly recall visiting the Queen's for an hour, then making my way unsteadily down the road to the 007 Club. Like Toulouse Lautrec, I was there only for the atmosphere. I was told it used to be a music hall, but by the time I got there little remained of all round family entertainment. The dimly-lit interior was home to comedians working the northern circuit, some better than others and all, I seem to recall, with shirt cuffs of such length they reached mid way down the backs of their hands. Occasionally these stalwarts of comedy made a joke not to the audience's taste and a contretemps would develop. The act would resume after an apology by the comedian and its acceptance by the punter. The 007 was also famous for its speciality female performers, who preferred to dance in the buff. These were usually ignored by gamblers in the back room, who were more intent on their winnings than anything going on in the adjacent performance area.

But I found the Jazz Club, which took place in the George Hotel, more to my taste than the others, and for a couple of years I made that my staple entertainment.

Perhaps on a sliding scale of 'respectability' the ballroom at Trentham Gardens would come out top. I only went there a couple of times, not because I was not respectable (in my opinion), but because it was far away and I seemed to have formed the notion that only Victor Sylvester acolytes would be welcome. Trentham was the natural venue of The Big Band, the full-flare dress and suit, pillars around which furtive men peeped and first cocktails. If you wanted to meet anyone who was anyone, that was where you went.

My dancing years phase came and went. And so did the venues. Where would my early education have been without them?

11. THE SANS-CULOTTE

But it wasn't all play. As a pupil, and later as a student, I had a variety of jobs. None were particularly hard to obtain; neither were they arduous in comparison with current working practice where an employee is expected to quote the company mantra in his sleep.

Like now, finding casual work relied on a mixture of nepotism and being in the right place at the right time. Thus a friend's sister found me employment descaling roof joists at Doulton's, an aunt put in a word at Woolworth's and I attached myself unaided to the Christmas Post and a miscellany of local dairies and bakeries.

The Safety Acts were less rigid then. At the Nile Street works I was handed not a hard hat, but a wire brush. Poised 30 feet above the concrete on a makeshift scaffold, three of us attacked the rust with vigour. It was Wakes, 1958, and the entire factory had departed for Rhyl, leaving we part-time maintenance men to brush away unsupervised. Presumably the girders would later be red-leaded, but not by us. We were the sans-culotte of the labour force, driven by that little manilla envelope which would see us through another term.

My aunt worked for the Home and Colonial in Tunstall Market Square, Woolworth's being just around the corner. She was friendly with the then Woolworth's cashier, Eva. Two years before my Doulton's job, Eva was kind enough to take me under her wing. I was issued with a beige overall and delegated to duties aloft in the stock department, an Aladdin's cave of everything from rolls of tinsel to boys' jumpers. It was far from the throng of week-end shoppers, an inner-sanctum pervaded by the smell of detergents and cardboard, of mouse-like rustlings and the occasional dim ping of cash registers from below. There must have been order; to me it appeared a jumble of merchandise, shelved, floored, suspended and draped without reason, an Eastern bazaar shrouded in gloom and mystery.

A year later I found weekend employent at a Stoke dairy. My job was to brush out the grids and stack up the empties. The system at that time was to shunt employees internally from job to job, the theory behind this being the avoidance of boredom and a corresponding increase in productivity. The bottle-washing team would be transferred to loading up, the loaders to bottle-washing, and me to search for slugs. For two mind-numbing hours at a stretch I encamped before a lens behind which marched an army of bottles straight from the wash. My mission was to look out for "foreign residues" and to remove the offending bottle. Slugs seemed the main culprit, able to survive the punishing cleaning routine with all their faculties intact.

Months later, with real experience behind me, I opted for a step up, working for a rival dairy closer to home. Now this was more to my taste. They put me on school deliveries and I sat alongside a lugubrious character known to everyone as Deakin in a brand new Ford truck. Up at 4.30am, loaded by six, we would leave the yard with our crates of one-third-of-a-pint bottles and do our drops throughout the city. We were back at base by the early afternoon. Deakin usually found "urgent business" to attend to while I unloaded the empties. He always magically put in an appearance as I was stacking the last of the crates on the loading deck. At this point I left him to hose down the wagon and cycled off home to bed.

It was the Christmas Post which appealed most. I loved to tramp the streets keeping a leisured, constant pace, until my deliveries were complete. I had no idea letterboxes could come in such a variety of styles and heights, or that they could be so absent from the houses to which most mail was directed. Several times I escaped injury by a hair's breadth as some snapping mongrel leapt at my fingers fumbling at the aperture. I soon got used to it and fed only cards to the dogs.

Then it was back to the Hanley depot, flushed pink by the winter and making a mental note of the tips received. Could I now afford the new saddlebag, or the shirt I'd seen in Burton's window? Not quite? Maybe I could persuade the old man to fork out.

The other day I met someone I used to teach. We stopped to chat and he told me that both he and his wife had given up well paid jobs to drive vans. They had made a conscious decision to forgo the increasing demands made by their respective employers on their free time.

When I was young, I worked to live. It was always the English way, with time for hobbies after the daily stint. The country's enormous inventive talent was released between seven and nine at night, with many a man producing scale models of A4 Pacifics in his shed and many a wife bespoke outfits which would put a professional to shame.

I wonder how long the Sino-American reverse will hold true in this country? Do you really need a Mission Statement to catch slugs in bottles?

12. BOW LEGS & KNOCK KNEES

Workers in the health professions were universally respected. Medical provision in the 1950s was not as antediluvian as some suppose. The Matron was the scourge of the hospital, and ran it with such frightening efficiency that even the doctors deferred to her rule book. Wards were spotless and woe betide the hapless nurse who fell short of Matron's exacting standards. She was nevertheless respected. In most cases she had devoted her life to medical care and knew hospitals inside out. If I were casting for the part of chief executive, Hattie Jacques would be the last person I would choose. Balancing the books is nowadays seen as the main palliative and from this perspective a background in nursing would seem a disadvantage.

The local GP played his part, in most cases entering into the spirit of the newly-formed National Health Service with commitment and vigour. Many other services complemented these provisions and liaised with firms, schools and other organisations to maintain a healthy regimen for employees and pupils alike.

At school I remember regular checks on weight and height, and frequent visits by ancillaries to make sure you were in 'full working order'. The school nurse would inspect your head for nits or ringworm. Flat feet, knock knees, bow legs and other such complaints were also cause for scrutiny. For any of these maladies a trip to the school clinic was prescribed, where more or less effective treatments were meted out.

From Ryan Hall clinic, situated next to Tunstall Railway Station in the then Station Road, emanated an odour of iodine so pungent the rickets sufferer felt less knock-kneed merely by entering the building. The curative properties of this miracle vapour wafting down the staircase was sufficient to dispel any doubts as to the efficiency of the treatments available in that crucible of modern medicine.

Here ears were poked, eyes tested, teeth examined, limbs strengthened, elementary osteopathy practised, cobblers of rectifying footwear summoned, advice dispensed and, if you were fortunate, nit combs issued. The small room was an alchemist's cell. Chemicals in brown jars lined the shelves, labelled pastes and ointments filled the recesses and bottles with glass stoppers were spread in seemingly haphazard array over every horizontal surface. This was Merlin's den, presided over by a gowned lady who no doubt worked for the great magician himself. Unfortunately, he never put in an appearance.

I was fortunate not to have to avail myself of much medical help in my early teens. Measles, scarlet fever, chickenpox and other complaints had passed me by. But there was still the occasional accident. One such occurred on a cycling trip. Returning home from a run, a friend and I took a short cut down the steeply sloping Peck Mill Lane, Brindley Ford. My bike wasn't the most up to date of machines, and its principal failing was in the brake department. I approached the hill with caution, but momentum took over. The brakes wouldn't hold and I careered downwards at an ever increasing speed. The lane turned sharply over a bridge at the base of the hill. Unable to control the bike, I negotiated only part of the bend before fate paid me a visit in the shape of a large tree. I remember the impact, followed by a crushing lethargy as I struggled to raise myself from the clump of nettles which had become my temporary home. The bike was a right-off, the front wheel buckled, the forks pushed far back towards the saddle.

My friend, who had seen it all and feared the worst, was surprised when I staggered onto the asphalt. Nevertheless, he took the precaution of running to a nearby bungalow to summon help. Luckily the man had a phone, and within a short time I was taken to hospital for a check-up. Happily nothing was amiss.

I found myself in a similar situation six years later, in 1959. The venue on this occasion was the cross-roads below Sneyd Hill, Smallthorne. This time I had failed to notice the lights had changed. I collided with a car coming across my path and travelled through the sky to land on the pavement some 10 yards away. Like the man in the film, I found myself looking up into a circle of concerned and silent faces. The ambulance was there within minutes and I was treated for abrasions. The bike survived.

I relate these anecdotes to demonstrate my experience of health practice then. While others may have a different story to tell, my family and I found much to admire in the health care of the time - free, as it was, from the constraints of global markets.

A MOSAIC OF MEMORIES

Included here are memories of the rites of passage I shared with others of my generation. As I progressed from flannels to drainpipes, I fantasised about acquiring a body of Greek proportions - my own, at least to begin with - and taming my disinterested thatch.

A menagerie of pets came and went, as did the 1947 winter. We ran through Coronation showers and walked, complaining, on Church processions through the terraced Tunstall streets.

We are told these were bleak days of privation. They never felt like it to me. Post War buoyancy was afoot, and I was a part of it.

Chapters

1. Clothes for the Boy (May 2002)

2. Short Trousers & Chapped Knees (Jan 1999)

3. A Pair of Drains (Oct 2000)

4. Acquiring a Good Body (April 1999)

5. Short Back & Sides (June 2003)

6. Sledging (Dec 1998)

7. Has He Been Yet? (Dec 1998)

8. The New Elizabethans (June 2002)

9. At the Mercy of the Elements (May 2003)

10. Cats & Dogs (Jan 2000)

11. A Nod, a Wink and a Song

1. CLOTHES FOR THE BOY

There's the sports jacket, the linen jacket, my bargain-price worsted winter jacket and the deconstructed jacket which makes me look like a Sicilian bandit. I don't wear the suits much, but they're there too. Then there are jeans, chinos, shoes and socks. Fifteen pairs, to be precise. And fifteen shirts. And they're just the short-sleeved ones. Their long-sleeved brethren are parked in an overspill wardrobe awaiting autumn. Then there's my George Raft mac, my waxed mac, my lightweight summer mac, my Austin Reed duffle mac, and much, much more besides. I'm a consumer junkie at heart, just like you.

As a child I shared a tallboy with my brother. It was a low, 1930s piece which still bore the pencil marks of some long forgotten carpenter. It had a brass rail and three small drawers which moved easily on their runners because there was rarely anything in them. Suspended from the rail were a few wire hangers. These, like the drawers, were usually devoid of clothing, although for a brief spell they had supported a couple of homemade flannel jackets.

I had two shirts, one grey, the other white. I wore them alternately. Monday was washing day and one or the other went with the family laundry into the copper. I never felt conspicuously poor. The neighbours' children were no better clad and at least my shirts were unpatched. You would have thought such deprivations would render me insensitive. Not so. I hated my itchy grey shirt with venom and would willingly put up with its unwashed companion forever. We are told the early Christian martyrs sought forgiveness through camel hair. They would have been more than willing to offer themselves to Beelzebub, hair-shirt and all, than to suffer an hour in my grey number.

I remember only one instance when my mother took me for 'an outfit'. I must have been around ten. The shop was situated in Tunstall Haymarket - a supermarket now occupies the site.

"I'd like clothes for the boy," my mother informed the tailor.

"Would that be a complete outfit, madam?"

"Everything but the shoes," she replied.

Being measured for new clothes was a novel experience. After a brisk and efficient interval, a neatly-folded collection of items rose from the counter. Shirt, jacket, underwear, short trousers, socks and Burberry. Sartorial audacity indeed.

Ironically, I was less impressed by my new wardrobe than by belt. Previously I had worn braces. Belts signified adulthood. They were a rite of passage. Their main purpose - keeping my trousers up - was incidental. The belt now being added to my stock was of patterned elastic, fastened with a snake clasp. Everyone else had a belt like that. Now it was my turn.

My adult status was later confirmed when I had my first pair of shoes. Before that, steel-shod boots had been my daily wear, with black plimsolls for summer. My shoes were style free, label free and came in black. For the first few days I kept them mirror-bright. They were my badge of office, like an RAF pilot's moustache or a priest's chasuble. But the novelty soon wore off. Although they hadn't reached the can-kicking stage, I grew lazy and began to ignore the increasingly scuffed toe-caps.

My brother, four years my junior, was the recipient of many a cast-off. My V-neck pullover came his way, as did the Burberry and what was left of my trousers. My two ties, mere tow-ropes, passed into joint ownership.

The transnationals hadn't latched on to brand names then. The fact you had something on your back was the only requirement. Holed footwear could be card-patched until the end of the week, when there might be money for the cobbler. Everything was makeshift, make-do-and-mend, patched, darned, worn to destruction and recycled. Coats became rag rugs. Old woollens reverted to skeins from which new knit-wear sprang. Shirts morphed to dusters. Anything left went to the rag and bone man. Even he was recycled.

Now I sort through my range of blue shirts. Which one today? I'm really bewildered. I'm Stressed Eric. Maybe there's something to be said for my two-shirt wardrobe of 50 years ago. Despite the itch.

2. SHORT TROUSERS & CHAPPED KNEES

In the Forties, a decent suit was a prized item. One wore it as Best, to be taken from the wardrobe only on Sundays and those Special Occasions which marked the year. One attended weddings and funerals done up in one's Best. And Hanley on Saturday mornings.

The rough worsted chafed the skin and the collar chafed the larynx, but you had moved up a notch and your social progress was defined by what you had on your back. My mother made my brother and me matching lumber jackets and short trousers. She had bought a grey serge from the market and knocked up the garments in two weekends from war-time patterns she had found in a drawer. I demanded an inside pocket and got one. Inside pockets were a token of adulthood and maturity. She also supplied breast pockets on the jackets, flapped and held by a single bone button. I liked my suit and wore it for Best, then for school, then for playing in.

What I couldn't abide was the grey shirt I had to tolerate when my other was in the copper. The sight of this shirt hanging on the kitchen rack was enough to send me into a fit of petulant misery. I don't know what it was made of, but the texture was such that my skin balked at its coarseness. I demonstrated my resistance by standing with sentry-like stiffness for a good 10 minutes after putting it on.

Eventually the shirt was discarded, as was the lumber jacket. At the same time my school plimsolls grew too small, my steel-shod boots began to pinch and I got the hang of knotting a tie.

My 1940s had been marked with the paraphernalia of slack garters and gravity-stricken socks, of short trousers and bruised knees, of V-necked pullovers and curled-up collars. But then I reached ten, and a new decade.

The first to go was the short trousers. A throw back to the middle-class Edwardian fashion of dressing up one's offspring in knickerbockers, short trousers were neither practical nor safe. They ensured cold legs in winter, chapped skin after rain and a constant affliction of cuts, abrasions and bruises. Short trousers were responsible for a scar I bear on my knee to this day, the result of tripping over an overgrown mineral line in Bradwell Wood and finding a broken bottle. I was glad to be rid of them.

My mother relented as Secondary School beckoned and I became the proud possessor of a pair of manly flannels. Thus was my rite of passage assured. I could now look down on those mortals who had fallen short of my sartorial apogee and stride to school comfortable in the knowledge that I could take my place in the Big Wide World - without plasters.

It was some time before I ventured into jeans, but in the mid-Fifties street fashions came of age. I was an innocent abroad, and it was on one of my excursions to Tunstall that I caught my first glimpse of the new exotic male. I saw him walking through the park. He was wearing a light grey suit with a dark collar, a string tie, red socks and suede shoes whose crepe sole must have increased his height by a couple of inches.

His crowning glory glistened with Brylcreem and swept from a bow-bob in front to a well-combed 'duck's arse' at the rear. When he passed me I affected a sudden interest in the bandstand. So this was the much vaunted Teddy Boy I had heard about.

I could never bring myself to emulate him, or the others I saw later. But I did give in slightly. My contribution was a pair of bilious green socks and beetle crushers which my feet never got used to lugging about. Nylon shirts with cutaway collars had come in and vests had gone out. So next time I went through Tunstall Park I felt my street cred was, if not totally intact, at least nodding in the right direction.

I grew bolder, with unfortunate results. A succession of paid Saturday morning jobs had enabled me to make a foray into what I deluded myself into thinking was "hip" clothing. As a teenager and in the company of two friends, I would descend on Burton's almost weekly and pick up an assortment of brightly-coloured and generally unwearable items. One Saturday afternoon the need to own a sports jacket suddenly presented itself to me. I had seen Bill Haley wear an oversized one with enormously padded shoulders and a flecky fabric that shrieked America.

I made the purchase - a louche, powder-blue ensemble capable of halting a convoy. I wore it once before deciding it was not for me. In the way of teenagers everywhere, I bought a packet of dye and dunked the offending garment into a charcoal-grey sink. Though I followed the instructions to the letter, the jacket I dragged from the water was not the one I put in. In the process of acquiring its new, understated hue, it had also shrunk to pigmy size and the once-proud shoulder pads had migrated to the elbow.

In those days, the rag-and-bone man was a regular visitor to the estate where I lived. When he next called, over his cart was draped my shrunken Bill Haley jacket, ignominious amid the scrap. You would think I would have learnt from the experience. Not so. Within the year I had purchased and discarded a three-piece Harris Tweed suit (my Baronial phase), a shirt in the same shade of pink as Jayne Mansfield's Cadillac and a pair of Jesus sandals. But I did stop short of the Teddy Boy suit. And the DA haircut.

'Shopping was an expedition': Tunstall Market Square, 1940s.

The paddling pool: Tunstall Park

3. A PAIR OF DRAINS

I had forgotten the green socks and crepes, when a recent visit to Hope Street rekindled my memory. I discovered Nowak's there in 1957. A boy called Dowd had introduced me to the name. Dowdy was the token school Ted. His natural inclinations curtailed by regimen, he asserted himself in areas the regulations hadn't yet reached. Thus he was able to get away with a Tony Curtis bob, cut-away collars and 15-inch trouser bottoms while we conformists played safe. He wore a blazer like the rest of us. And his trousers were of grey flannel as demanded by the school code book. But he had had them tapered, and that is where Nowak's came in.

Sartorially, schools have always been at odds with their times. Hanley High School was no different. The anachronistic blazer, cap and flannels affronted our sense of style. My first task when I got home was to discard them in favour of something I hoped would enhance my presence in the locality. Unfortunately I was a late developer. My trouser bottoms still flapped around my ankles - until I met Dowd, that is.

"You want to pay a visit to Nowak's. He'll see you right."

"What does he do, then?"

"He'll take 'em in for you. He does whatever size you want."

"What are yours?"

"These are 15s. I've got a pair of drains at home and they're only 12-inch."

From Dowdy's edited highlights, I eventually managed to glean the facts: Nowak was a tailor with a business in Hope Street, Hanley. If you presented him with a regulation pair of flannels he would be happy to taper the bottoms to Teddy Boy width for only a few bob. It seemed at the time that most of Nowak's income was derived from Ted manques who sought to improve their weekend status by gartering their ankles in trousers which were virtually circulation-proof.

So one Saturday I caught the bus to town, my spare trousers in a carrier and a nagging doubt in my head. What if he wrote the trousers off? What if he didn't cut them right, just pinched in the bottoms cycle-clip fashion? What if he tapered them severly to the knees and left the upper half to its own devices? Jodhpurs were not something I coveted. Who was this man? Had Dowdy been winding me up?

I found the shop, inconspicuous in the row. Hesitantly I entered. A small polished counter with an inlaid brass rule faced me. Chalk-marked jackets in various stages of construction occupied gloomy corners. A smell of fabric hung in the air. Then a velvet curtain swished aside and Mr Nowak himself materalised from a back room.

"I've brought some trousers to be tapered," I offered lamely, spilling the bag's contents on to the counter. He prodded them disinterestedly. "What size?" I thought I might take a leaf out of Dowd's book and plump for 12-inch, but I doubted I would get them over my size 11s.

"15-inch," I volunteered.

"You might be in trouble there. You're a tall lad. Why not have 18s?"

He uncoiled a tape from his neck and applied it to a leg.

"You see? That would be 18 inches. It would allow you a bit more freedom."

I was doubtful. Cred was size-related. I had to consider my image.

"I'd prefer 17-inch," I mumbled, determined to make a stand. He shrugged and dropped the trousers into the bag. "Call next week. I'll have them ready for you."

By 10.00 the following Saturday the newly-tapered trousers had been bagged and collected. Half my week's pocket money had gone into the venture and I couldn't help wondering if the whole thing hadn't been a mistake. When I got in, I went immediately to my room and removed Mr Nowak's modification from its wrapping. I held the flannels aloft and ran my eyes over the newly narrowed legs. With trepidation I began to pull the trousers on, shoe-horning the bottoms over my stockinged feet, fearful lest the tailor's handiwork suffered in the process.

I regarded myself in my parent's cheval. Max Wall would have felt at home in them. I turned sideways, admiration vying with embarrassment at the sight of my hideously jutting feet. Dowdy's immaculate taperings had suited him. But he was only five feet eight, with size 9s to match. I was 6ft 1in, with shoes the size of tennis rackets. I was not sure I had been well advised after all. And I was down on my pocket money. It was some time before I plucked up the courage to go downstairs. I took care not to mention my excursion into haute couture to my parents. They would discover it soon enough. And by that time the fashion for drainpipes might have changed. At least I hoped so. In fact, it couldn't come soon enough.

4. ACQUIRING A GOOD BODY

Acquiring strange clothes was not the sole idiosyncrasy of my teenage years. My desire to cultivate a body which would do justice to the items I bought - and quickly discarded - also loomed large in the scheme of things.

Although my father frowned at the editorial direction of The News of the World, a copy was always available on the Sunday table. And it was there, tucked away in a page conspicuous with advertisements for everlasting roses and corn cures, that I first met Charles Atlas. Mr Atlas's teeth were so even he appeared to be wearing a gum shield. He must have thought Sundays a joke, for whenever I found him he wore a constantly beaming smile. He always posed so that his pectoral muscles eclipsed any doubt I might have harboured that he was, indeed, flesh and blood. If you tilted his picture sideways in a good light you could make out a set of abdominals so defined they could have been mistaken for a topographical map of the Peak District.

Mr Atlas had a New Method. No more weights, dumbbells or bench presses. Instead he would teach me how to look like him using his method for just a few minutes a day. No apparatus at all. No longer would I be the guy who got sand kicked in his face. Now I could do the kicking. Just a few minutes a day. That was all it took.

The method involved a strict diet and the use of one's bodily reserves of latent strength. Instead of using weights, you pressed. If huge biceps were what you coveted, you simply applied the downward force of your right palm to your left and pressed with might and main. Or vice versa. To achieve outstanding abdominals you had to trap your toes under a mangle and rise like a mummy from a sarcophagus for an increasing number of times per week. I tried each of the exercises in my bedroom with no success. I was six feet one and weighed less than 11 stone. I wanted to be six feet one and have the sort of body he promised me, with deltoids I could take off and fly with. Nightly I measured my biceps. I even cheated with the tape. After six months of pointless contortions I increased my right bicep by a quarter of an inch. My left one refused to budge. I was a wimp. I could already feel the sand in my face.

But I was not to be defeated. I left Charlie to gather dust under the bed and adopted Scheme Two. This involved sending for a pint bottle of some nostrum "absolutely guaranteed" not only to render your body Herculean, but to increase your weight in a matter of weeks by more than 20 per cent. I rushed my application for 'Power Surge' to a London address and received a bottle some weeks later. I was to take a tablespoonful of the contents three times a day. According to the blurb, it was packed full of essential vitamins and supplements my body was incapable of manufacturing under its own steam. I consumed three bottles of this ghastly stuff and by careful daily weighing was able to confirm my fears: I had lost about five pounds during the course of treatment.

Still undeterred, I decided that weights were the thing and that I had been duped by both Charles and Power Surge. Alas, I was unable to afford so much as a dumbbell. I thought friends who waxed long about the Greek ideals of proportion might have a set of weights I could borrow. They hadn't. One or two were still struggling with Mr Atlas, and would undoubtedly come round to my own view in the event of a rupture.

However, I eventually acquired what to me was as good as the most sophisticated weights set on the market. This device was not unlike a mattress spring and came complete with an instruction book promising, as before, that I would in days acquire such power I would be capable of kicking sand into the faces of every man on the beach simultaneously if I fettered myself to the programme.

And that is where I came unstuck. For one of the exercises involved an elaborate bicep routine whereby it was necessary to trap the spring under your foot and, gripping the handle firmly, flex it towards your face. I felt sufficiently confident to attempt this feat with three springs attached, the maximum the stretcher allowed. Up to my bedroom I crept, embarrassed in case anyone knew what I was up to. Carefully I trapped the spring under my foot and began to heave. There was an almighty thud. I felt as if my nose had collided with the wall. When I came to, the discarded spring lay on the bed where it had fallen, snapped in half.

I stroked my nose gingerly. It seemed to be in two sections, the parts separated by a lump the size of a robin's egg. My head swam. I eased myself down to think. When I felt better I opened the window and threw out the spring, Charlie's grinning face, and the remaining contents of my Power Surge. There was to be no more body building for me. Who wanted 20 inch biceps anyway? And I hardly ever went to the beach.....

5. SHORT BACK & SIDES

I never seemed to stick with one barber. The field had to be played, and though the cramped and generally dowdy rooms from which they operated had much in common, there was just enough variety to make exploration worthwhile.

Some premises still bore the symbol of the tonsorial art. This was a pole some three inches in diameter with red and white stripes running helter-skelter down its length. It would be conspicuous above the door and leave the seekers of haircuts in no doubt that they had arrived at the right place. By the late 1950s, however, these traditional emblems had all but disappeared. Instead there were black and white posters advertising Brylcreem above the well-groomed head of some smiling sportsman, usually a cricketer, since cricket was perceived as a gentleman's game and only gentlemen would sport the sort of barnet of which Brylcreem approved.

I gravitated to these emporiums of the hirsute from the back yard, where for a time my mother had given me a quick trim using dressmaking scissors and a head-sized bowl. The results were not quite in the Cary Grant class, but who knows - perhaps in his former incarnation as Archibald Leech even Cary's mother did the same for him.

My first visits to the hairdresser must have coincided with my earning some part-time money. I discovered my main man in one of the side streets off Smallthorne Bank and he set the trend for much of what followed. His 'salon' had once been a front parlour. It retained the dilapidated air of a house which had fallen on hard times. A pile of tatty periodicals sat on the torn leather upholstery; the one window was grey with grime, the boards stained ebony.

The barber, a spare figure of twitching eye and nervous hand, presided over a brace of high wooden chairs which, like their owner, had seen better days. His talent lay in reducing the range of available styles to two: 'brush' cut, or short back and sides. His conversation was equally limited, consisting of an introductory comment on the weather, an inquiry regarding your choice of style and a parting shot regarding your supposed girlfriend. Something along the lines of: "Yer'll 'ave t' fend 'er off, mate. 'er'll be all over yer tonight."

His long silences were punctuated by drags on a cork-tip whose finger of ash lengthened to gravity-defying proportions as he worked. By some feat of levitation he was able to keep the ash suspended until the inevitable happened and it exploded down your neck. At this point a mumbled apology was offered and a paintbrush produced, which he would use to wipe away the offending grains.

I usually opted for short back and sides. In his case this meant no sides and little top save for a Rin Tin Tin quiff which stood erect like a cock's comb. The effect was enhanced by the sort of hair oil Victor Mature must have used in his beefcake Old Testament epics. It was applied from a de-corked bottle using the then popular palming method. The hairdresser would pour a quantity into his open palm and apply it directly to your scalp whether or not you'd requested it.

From time to time I opted for a brush cut and emerged looking like a hopeful auditioning for a chorus part in South Pacific. He was just beginning to get the hang of a Tony Curtis bob and, what had by then become commonplace among his rivals, a DA, when the time came for us to part.

It was to be some years before these shrines to the thatch were dragged into the 20th century. By the late 1960s, the strop and cut-throat had largely been relegated to the waste bin, the new man was no longer a barber but a *stylist*, and the customer had more of a say in his appearance. "I want to look like him," you would mumble, pulling out a well-creased photograph of Yul Brynner. "No problem, mate. It might take some time."

Now I visit my hairdresser and a new shorthand has developed. No longer a disciple of short back and sides or brush cut, this man relies only on numbers. I've more or less got the hang of it, even to the extent of requesting interesting combinations. A two on top and five at the sides - like Richard III, for example. I've not yet asked to be shaved bald. Nature will see to that soon enough. Predictably, even baldness is subject nowadays to insider jargon. They call it a 'bic job', apparently. Maybe we've not come so far after all.

6. SLEDGING

Someone had died in one of the steel-framed houses. I had taken a back-street route from school and was about to turn into our road when I caught a looming shape out of the corner of an eye. I had seen funeral cars before, vast black limousines, their inward curving rear reminiscent of the horse-drawn hearses of 50 years earlier. But this car was different; not in looks, but in the way it was gliding towards me across the ice. While the car was spinning, the mourners gazed lugubriously through the windows. It would have been inappropriate for them to shriek warnings to the driver. It was a time to bear stoically what was in store and would have spoilt the moment. The driver, lugubrious as the rest, could do nothing to arrest the car's progress across the tarmac. It drew alongside me as I gained the shelter of the street-lamp, and continued its silent back-to-front journey until it reached the main road.

I suppose such events were commonplace during the '47 winter. At least when the roads were open. High Lane was narrowed by drifts, Bemmersley Lane impassable, Loop Line services reduced to a Sunday minimum. Wells' buses steamed up Pittshill, but Arthur's slat-seated Bedford could no longer climb Greenbank Road and the milkman stumbled with the dailies.

My father dug a path to the gate. The snow was piled on either hand to the height of my head and stretched in a vast plane to the lattice fence, which appeared as a dark trace in the tyre slush. Mounds covered sills and panes. The door swelled and stuck. In the morning, fresh falls mocked the previous day's labour. Salt was sprinkled until there was no more left to buy and McGough's struggled to deliver fuel to our coalshed.

Close to our house, a rim of steep-sided hills overlooked a quarry which since the 1930s had been used as a dump. While the corporation carts struggled with their loads, we struggled with our sledges. Everyone seemed able to procure a sledge at a moment's notice. Many were elaborate affairs boasting greased steel runners and seating for three. Those who had no sledge hitched a lift on someone else's or made do with a sack. The venue was the steepest part of the hill, which also offered the greatest chance of concussion. My sledge, like the three-wheeled trolley I had acquired a few months earlier, was a cobbled-together assortment of struts and timber remnants. It weighed a ton, and it was a moot point whether the effort involved in hauling it to the top of the slope was worth the run down, with the additional risk of a cracked patella.

It must have been. I dragged my conveyance resolutely up the side on scores of snowless afternoons and slid into dusk and disaster with monotonous regularity. It was expected that at least one participant would part company with his sledge on his descent. The chance of this happening was increased by a perilously-sited hump just beyond the foot of the hill. It lay buried beneath a layer of snow and toppled me on many occasions. Those whose transport was quicker off the mark acquired the respect of their slower peers in being catapulted into the air at this point, and a member of the fraternity would frequently be forced to capitulate and bear his scars homeward.

The winter reached interminably into spring. We endured power cuts and broken shovels, chapped hands and heatless fires. Yet our spirits remained indominatable. My father told us that helicopters had dropped supplies to Moorland farmers. I did not know what Moorland meant, and was only vaguely aware what constituted a helicopter through seeing one in the Picture Post. Yet the word Moorland had the sinister ring one came to associate with remote territories overseas.

The thaw seemed even harsher than the winter. The nine-foot drifts which had blanketed the waste tips yielded slowly to the spring sun, and the air bore an intense chill. The wind moaned in the bath overflow, the sledge was relegated to the shed, then to the fire. Red tiles showed through the white and the last tattered remnants of the season gave way to the first flowers.

There have been colder winters, perhaps longer winters. But the winter of 1947, paying us an unwelcome visit within one year of finding a house of our own, was the one I remember most vividly.

7. HAS HE BEEN YET?

My young Christmases were a mixture of nail-biting anticipation, snowball fights, nipped fingers and feverish excitement. The crib was out at school, with whisps of grass in the manger and the plaster figures of Joseph, Mary and the Infant dusted off for the season and made to stand in a corner for days on end.

When Santa wasn't in Lapland, he had a grotto in Lewis's basement. A fairy holding a foil-wrapped star accompanied him while a crocodile of hopefuls filed in. She wore a scowl and looked more like Santa's minder than the Herald of Christmas. No glad tidings there. Santa, on the other hand, eked out his pension dispensing bonhomie to the claimants. He was overlooked by mothers whose smiles faded in anticipation of their off-spring's demands. After all, this was Father Christmas. He could get anything. His pixies could knock up a Hornby train set in two minutes flat. There was nothing too expensive, no chimney too small to cram it all down. Santa had them sitting one by one on his knee. Nowadays he would be arrested for child abuse.

"Hello, and what's your name, little girl?"

"Jennifer Mary Scott."

"And what d'you want for Christmas, my dear?"

"I'd like a three-wheeler bike with a box for carrying my teddy and a doll that cries real tears and an Enid Blyton Annual and a new party frock."

"Is that all? What colour frock would you like?"

"Pink with white edging."

Santa would simper into his stick-on beard while Jennifer departed and the queue shuffled forward, the Good Fairy preventing a crush by using her wand as a barricade. Sometimes he left his lair for a PR job around the streets. I saw him once struggling through the High Lane snow atop a coach and four. He looked frozen, and had wrapped up his trousers in a khaki blanket, probably from the Surplus shop. He had four jolly Dickensians with him who swayed precariously all the way to Chell and back, taking it in turns to ring a handbell which had a curious Pied Piper effect on every child they passed.

The days gathered pace. At home the family worked feverishly, producing decorations from flour-pasted chains of colour paper which were then tacked from corner to corner with drawing pins. I don't remember a tree. But there were balloons which survived the Twelve Days attached to the picture rail in groups of three.

The ritual began. First, the argument with my brother regarding Santa's existence, followed by his constant appeal to my parents to "tell me the truth." My father was vehement in his denials that Santa was other than who he purported to be. Indeed, I think he half believed in him himself until the day he died. Then came the "wait and see" phase, wherein we bombarded my mother and father with "What are we having for Christmas?" though we had confirmed the books and boots stacked against the spare room wall weeks back.

On Christmas Eve I went to bed early and couldn't sleep. When I heard my father lugging my second-hand Raleigh up the stairs I closed my eyes and feigned slumber until the pillow case had been stuffed and he retreated. It was a long time till dawn and my brother's waking query: "Has he been yet?" But I didn't let on who "he" was. I didn't let on that *I knew*.

Christmas Day rang with bells and I rode my bike through the slush, grew chillblains and wolfed my Mars Bar. Relations came around, or we went to them. It was some time before I realised uncles weren't always the laughing, word-slurring people I'd met at Christmas. And that their maudlin fare was the stuff of festivities everywhere.

"We won't leave it so long next time."

"No, you're welcome any time, any time."

The potters were back after a couple of days, the bike was laid up because of the snow and the Magic Fairy's silver wand was boxed and stored ready for next Christmas. By the Twelfth Day my mother had got fed up with re-gluing the streamer chains that had broken and stripped the walls back to their pre-festive condition. We scoffed the rest of the food, grew sick of blancmange and longed for meat and two veg again.

I grew into the bike and learned to ride with both legs over the crossbar. My brother ripped his team colours, punctured his football and shelved the question of Santa's identity for another year.

8. THE NEW ELIZABETHANS

A couple of weeks before the Queen's Coronation we were informed by our teacher we were in for a treat. We were to go on an afternoon excursion to Barber's Picture Palace, Tunstall, to see a film marking the significance of the great event. We in the Secondary Modern section of Hanley High School would march alongside our more academic peers all the way from Chell. We were ordered to enjoy ourselves. After the film, we were free to make our own way home.

After lunch, and under a mackerel sky threatening rain, we formed a crocodile which stretched from the school gates to Turnhurst. The throng attenuated along Victoria Park Road, making it difficult for masters to keep an eye open for any who might care less for regal splendour than for the chance of a boating trip around the park lake.

We arrived as the first shower fell. The entire cinema was taken up by our numbers. On this occasion we and the grammar school lads were invited to share the rows, a rare democracy which was consolidated before the film by the issue of vanilla tubs to the wearers of jerseys and blazers alike.

Our treat was a eulogy to Britain. The lights dimmed, the curtains parted and our heritage was thrown across the screen in glorious Technicolor. We were the first of the New Elizabethans. We were proud of our standing in the world. We had won the war. Our jets could break the sound barrier. Edmund Hillary would conquer Everest that year. We were on the way to nuclear power. And the world's first jet airliner. And the world's first computer. We had given the world so much.

The camera panned across a quintessential English landscape dotted with the emblems of monarchical continuity: fort, village church and green, Cornish coves misty with salt spray, a sun-dappled Thames and the dreaming spires of Oxford. Shakespeare was in on the act too. Whenever he sensed a lull in the Vaughan Williams, Olivier would come to the playwright's aid to make sure we had grasped the complete picture: *'this happy breed of men, this little world, this precious stone set in a silver sea, this blessed plot, this earth, this realm, this England'.*

Union Jacks, real or imaginary, accompanied my homeward journey. My young mind was struggling to grapple with an unknowable awe. The

Queen was soon to be enthroned. Momentous changes were afoot.

My father signalled these by the acquisition of a television set and enrolment on the local festivities committee. What more could be done besides the mugs and bunting? The answer was street parties. The end of hostilities was still fresh in people's minds. Street parties held fond memories of pride and survival. So sub-groups were convened to organise them. In the event it rained and alternative arrangements were hastily put into action. This involved the youngsters in our street being invited into willing households to pursue Coronation pastimes there. I'm not sure what happened in other houses, but I remember the eight or so who had found their way into our house and who spent the time mutely gawping at the unfamiliar screen.

It brightened later in the afternoon and there were races in a bowl of grassed land near the tip. There was a fancy dress parade in the street. My father officiated at the races and prizes were awarded. I vaguely remember taking part in a sack race, but nothing came my way. My sister fared better in the fancy dress parade. My mother had been up until late the night before making my sister's fairy costume, a tutu with sequins and a wand from a garden cane.

My brother, keen to get in on the act, insisted on appearing dressed as a Roman. Raided wardrobes produced a discarded corset which, with its bits of whalebone and hook-ups, could be made to pass for an unrecorded item of gladiatorial dress. My father, never dextrous in practical matters, nevertheless managed to fashion a sword out of a couple of pieces of rough wood. The piece de resistance was the helmet. This strange survival had joined the family heirlooms via a long forgotten route, and consisted of stout leather thongs intertwined to form a kind of protective head-gear. The Roman soldier was thus born. He declined to fall on his sword when he failed to win a prize. However, other prizes were awarded, and, as more rain threatened, my mother's workmanship was rewarded. My sister's fairy won a doll.

The day passed. Richard Dimbleby had informed the nation that the Queen was duly enthroned. The potters returned to work and we to school. My ideas of nationhood, inchoate, unquestioning and naive, were embodied in that day, in its pageantry, in my brother's wooden sword, in the bunting at the window and the trek to the cinema. For a brief moment my world had extended further than Whitfield Colliery and the clanking engines which ran beneath it.

Such balm no longer exists, though we continue to fight for it, or a memory of it. In this harsher, infinitely more cynical world, I mourn the passing of those early securities of which the Queen's Coronation was a fitting emblem.

Tunstall - a vibrant town. Station Road, renamed The Boulevard.
Photo taken in the early 1950s

Coronation Day - and fancy dress parties.

9. AT THE MERCY OF THE ELEMENTS

Today was the day of the procession. I had a vague idea I was acceptable to God only so long as I was packaged in my 'Sunday Best.' My 'Sunday Best' was sacrosanct, and spent the greater part of its life mothballed in the tallboy. Today, however, my short trousers, jacket, shirt, vest, pants, socks and shoes were about to be released from captivity.

Tie and socks were members of the awkward squad. I had acquired a rudimentary knowledge of tie fixing by this time, but things didn't always go according to plan. I invariably gave up the struggle at an early stage and allowed the narrow end to assume its rightful place six inches below the wider and tucked into the top of my trousers, occasionally into my underpants.

Socks were equally precarious and ostracisation was the outcome of slack, wrinkly or holed ones. The unforgivable sin was to wear one sock higher than the other. In fact, the whole area of sockmanship (coupled with bedfellows short trousers and grazed knees) could prove a trap for the unwary. A key element was gartering. Garters were cut from a length of white elastic and knotted around the upper calf. Any surplus tape could be snipped off and my grey hosiery hauled to the knee and rolled back. The inch turndown thus formed hid the garter. If, in your quest for precision, you had pulled a hole in your stocking top, it hid that too.

The Procession always demanded bright boots, and these had normally been attended to the night before. Our brushes were worn to the wood and blackened with Cherry Blossom. A polishing rag was always on hand to burnish the leather to a gloss. Thus shod, I could ply the parish route with confidence. The Procession was an afternoon affair, kicking off at two sharp. It always seemed to take place on a cold Sunday, the sort of day that hadn't quite come to terms with the fact spring had arrived. We congregated by the church, an occasional curate in tow, the tall brass cross propped unceremoniously by the wall awaiting the last of the throng.

At quarter to two we shuffled into a rough file and prepared to offer ourselves to the elements. We would follow the parish boundary as well as we could. In the case of St Mary's, Tunstall, our route would take us up Lime Street to Booth Street, Sneyd Street and Clay Hills. We would return to the church via the High Street, the journey lasting less than a couple of hours.

Lost in the column of marchers, I nevertheless felt conspicuous in my elasticated best and Burberry and made sure I wasn't on the flank. The others seemed unconcerned - avid for action, even. Mothers' Union banners were unfurled and hoisted aloft by tweed-skirted matriarchs. In their wake trailed members of the Sunday School, following them surplice-clad choristers, their cheeks apple-bright in the chilling air. Bringing up the rear was the Reverend Cornes. The cross, now retrieved, was the highest ornament in the procession, held aloft and embellished, rather than outflanked, by the servers with their unlit candles.

The occasion needed music. Whether it got it or not seemed to depend on congregational contacts. Usually, an ensemble was produced, though from where, and who decided the repertoire, remains a mystery. As the time drew near, the cornetists, buglers and drummers took their place at the head of the line. A brief roll on the side drums, a booming response from the big bass drum and we were off past the Railway Tavern, the vicarage and my grandmother's house, plodding purposefully in the direction of the oatcake shop. We had reached the coal yard before the bunched participants had attenuated to form a 'proper' procession. The beat of the big drum announced our progress, cornets and bugles imparting a militaristic air at odds with the spiritual regeneration the vicar hoped the procession would accomplish.

The Procession always drew people to their doors. Onlookers' faces betrayed a range of emotions. Some were vaguely curious, others vaguely dismissive. Some were just vague. Toddlers, gripping their mother's skirts, understood only that they were witnessing something different, and this something was called 'The Procession.'

Thus we threaded our way through the terraced streets. The banners rippled in the heatless sun, a bugler blew a couple of tricky notes and wiped his nose. The big drum's booming announcement accompanied the crocodile and - who knows - uplifted the Reverend Cornes' spirits when he was in danger of flagging.

We usually got back to the church as the first drops fell. Perhaps a celestial Michael Fish was at work, rewarding us far all the hard work and the punishing schedule we had been set. As for me - well, all I could think of was getting my procession clobber back to the tallboy ASAP. Irreverent? Possibly.

10. CATS & DOGS

My family were never great pet lovers, but over the years by accident or caprice we were home to an assortment of animals. When I say we were not pet lovers, we didn't actively *dislike* animals. In fact, the opposite is nearer the truth. But to do justice to an animal's welfare takes time, money and patience, and though we had the latter to some degree, the other two were harder to find.

The first pet which inflicted itself upon us was an oil-soaked moggy. The cat had met with disaster on one of its nocturnal prowls around Pinnox Street, Tunstall, and would have no doubt come to an untimely end had it not been for the rescue service we provided. We found the creature on the doorstep one Sunday morning. We had no idea whose it was or how it had become contaminated with the glutinous sludge which bedraggled it.

My mother took it in and decided a galvanised tub of soapy water would restore the tom to health. The cat made no resistance, no doubt having spent its energy in an effort to escape the vessel into which it must have fallen. But the experiment proved a failure and we resorted to turps instead. It took several bottles before Sooty, as the cat was inevitably christened, was restored to full working order. He adopted us for many weeks after, no doubt happy in the knowledge a ninth life had been granted at the 11th hour.

When we moved to our new house in 1946 we became once more pet free. That was until the scrap man paid us a call. He made his presence felt at least once a month and on this occasion decided to risk venture capital on a crate of chicks. The birds were heart-rending bribes, of course, meant to induce importunate children to demand their parents part with their cooking utensils in exchange for a fluffy pet. It certainly worked with me. The rag and bone man received a defunct copper worth a few bob; in return I received a chick worth a few pence.

The chick quickly made itself at home and was given free rein of the downstairs rooms. It decided to adopt my mother and devoted its days to keeping a critical eye open for any shortcomings in her housework routine. When she cleaned the floor, the chick followed the mop. When she dusted the furniture, the chick pecked at the duster. It shadowed her everywhere and avoided death underfoot only by good fortune. Then one morning, instead of the reedy chirruping we had grown used to, there was silence. My father pronounced pneumonia and offered it whisky and water in a saucer. It took a feeble sip and rallied for an hour or two. My father's contention that there were few ailments a slug of Bell's couldn't cure didn't seem so far fetched after all. But then the end came, and our second pet was dispatched with ceremony to a plot below the line prop.

Then came the dog. Sandy was an uncoordinated, lolloping mongrel whose idea of canine bliss was to sink his teeth into the postman's leg. No amount of training had the least effect on this dog. It was difficult to impose a regimen on him since he ignored all commands. He was out of control, out of order and eventually out of the house, given away to a local dog-lover who thought he could 'do something with him'. In my mind's eye I carry a picture of Sandy's leave taking. He didn't seem the least concerned at his departure, and was leaping on to the back of his new owner with an abandon normally reserved for dogs less than half his age.

Later, as Sandy was becoming a distant memory, Scratch arrived. Scratch was a gnarled warrior-tom, the survivor of many battles with scars to prove it. He first took up residence in our shed and eventually smarmed his way into the house. His coat had seen better days, his ear was minus a chunk and he was probably psychotic. We never entirely got used to his mood swings. It was always dangerous to disturb him during sleep, and his sleep usually lasted the entire day. Indistinguishable from the remnant-woven hearth rug, his slumber was characterised by spasms and the occasional wail. When he was tripped over, which was often, he would instantly leap a couple of feet into the air, hair on end, claws out, what was left of his ears erect and attack whatever was within reach.

He was independent to the point of churlishness, but retained a spirit of adventure which eventually cost him his life. My mother found him in the coal shed, his back broken from fallen coal and miaowing piteously. He was taken to a Tunstall vet and put down. We all missed him.

After Scratch's departure, my father vowed there would be no more pets. I did win a goldfish which I bore home from a fair in a jar, but we didn't count this strictly as a pet since it was oblivious to our existence. Of course, my father didn't keep his word. When I married and left the family home, a new pet was purchased. A dachshund called Tosca. And she lived to a ripe and comfortable old age.

11. A NOD, A WINK, & A SONG

There was freedom from angst in the 1950s. People were happier. My mother sang *If You Were the Only Girl In the World* as she soaped the floor; the window cleaner whistled as he chammied the windows; bricklayers' raised their voices in a tuneless chorus from the scaffolding of unfinished houses. Perhaps the end of war had stimulated this catharsis. We had wiped the slate clean. Despite rationing, and what would now be termed privation, we were on the mend, rebuilding, optimistic. We were certainly at ease with ourselves, confident of a brighter future, secure in a national identity which had been reinforced, rather than shaken, by our part in hostilities.

From the contemporary perspective, there's no reason why we should have been happier then than now; in fact, the opposite might legitimately be claimed. Few owned cars and travelling anywhere was a chore. Houses were rented in the main, not owned. One had only one's work clothes and Sunday Best. Socks were darned on a mushroom and trousers patched at the seat. Central heating was not widely available, computers were almost unknown and video games were decades away.

So why did my mother sing into her suds-filled bucket and even my normally lugubrious father rise to the occasion with something from the Student Prince? Or am I imagining the amalgam of peace, humour, tolerance, good will and inner security which made up this elusive happiness? I don't think I am. Critics might argue that it's all a matter of age. Everyone was happier in his youth, they will say. Youth has no cares, no responsibilities. Ipso facto, youth is happy, old age less so. But this is not born out by the facts as I knew them as a teenager, and later as a teacher.

I began my teaching career in a small Junior school in 1960 and survived thirty seven years to retire as a Head of Department in a city comprehensive. Without doubt, a typical class of, say, 11-year-olds, was infinitely happier at the start of my career than at the end, whatever the yardstick used. By and large, the classes I taught in the sixties were receptive, calm, orderly, polite, enjoyed a joke, had a sense of fair play, manifested good will and were unlikely to be bored or distracted. For my own part, as a young teacher I knew what was expected of me and the rules were few and simple: keep order, keep them busy, impart whatever information you deem to be useful in digestible chunks.

By the time I finished full-time teaching in 1997, few of these descriptions were appropriate. Pupils were likely to be unhappy rather than happy, recalcitrant rather than orderly, rude, disinterested and frequently disturbed. There were exceptions, as there always will be, but generally this tendency to insecurity was tangible. And the comforting simplicities of professional life gave way to a quotidian mire of meetings, target setting, checklists, disciplinary procedures and exhaustion - hardly the stuff of contentment.

My early life was spacious enough to allow time for a joke, a smile, a nod, a wink, a song. It is testament to the strength of the English character that we haven't been destabilised in the mad scramble of contemporary life, a life that is incomparably more fraught than it used to be. Happiness is the bedfellow of freedom of thought, commitment to a common culture and security in home and work. The obverse breeds resentment, anxiety and bad faith despite the trappings of greater material well being.

I used to sit on my grandfather's chaise-longue watching the wreathes of smoke from his pipe dissipate against the ceiling. The only sound was the soporific tick-tock of his hand-me-down wall clock. An exquisite peace reigned. As my mother would say, "God's in His Heaven and All's Right with the World." There were many such moments in my boyhood. It was not hard to find peace, whether in my grandparent's blue-brick yard or on the grass colonised tips of the former colliery. Sounds were isolated in pockets; the hum of an aircraft, the 'thud, thud' of some distant machine. The noise saturation we tolerate today, and which adds to the stress of modern living, was largely absent.

A particular interlude sticks unaccountably in my mind. One day in the late 1940s I found myself lying amid the hummocks in an area of previously mined land close to our new home. Skylarks were attracted to this field in great numbers, and my gaze was arrested by one of these birds. It seemed unbelievable to me as a child that this infinitesimal speck could pour such cadences into the summer air and for so long. The minutes passed, but they seemed a suspension of real time, and brought a serenity which transcends orthodox religion. I remember it like yesterday. As I remember my mother's song, the window-cleaner's warblings and the musical overtures of men going about their work.

WINTER TALES

The writing in this section - two poems, two short stories and a piece I wrote for the Millenium edition of T*he Way We Were* - are all rooted in the experiences of my family and the history of the Potteries.

I have included them as a postscript to the preceding non-fiction which you have now hopefully worked through. I hope you have enjoyed sharing my reminiscences - and leave you with these final offerings.

Chapters

1. A Century of Change (Jan 2000)

2. A Fifties Christmas (Dec 2001)

3. A Sixties Christmas (Dec 2002)

4. The Watch (Nov 2000)

5. The Last Firing (Nov 1998)

1. A CENTURY OF CHANGE

It is summer, 1999. I am sitting on the balcony of a five star hotel. My room is air conditioned, and the floor is of marble. At a touch of the button I am able to select from eight TV channels. One is American, one British, one German, one Italian, two Greek, one French and one Spanish. I have just chosen a meal from a vast range of food. My room is provided with a phone. I can ring hotel reception, or anywhere else in the world.

My grandfather, who spent his life in Tunstall, was 33 before he saw the sea. The Irish Sea, not the Aegean. My father had never been abroad.

I'm neither particularly well-off nor poor in contemporary Western terms. My grandfather would have considered me rich as Croesus, as he would the other 500 people at the hotel. He would have been understandably surprised to know most were from what the sociologists used to call the C1 group, skilled manual workers. He would have been even more surprised to find that the British and Germans shared their accommodation amicably, that both were part of a European Union, and that their glory days on a world stage now dominated by America had long since faded.

There was an inkling even in my grandfather's time that the British Empire might not endure the onslaught of the parvenu New World. But these islands were not to be written off so quickly as a mere adjunct to the American Century. British inventiveness continued to hold its own, giving the world the jet engine, the first jet airliner, television, the hovercraft, the radio receiver, the microwave, Viagra, the Beatles, Mary Quant, Dolly, the discovery of DNA, the computer, the calculator, penicillin, nuclear fission, the light bulb, the video game and Cary Grant. To name just a few.

Yet the sense of an English identity, which my grandparents took for granted, has become confused in the last years of the century despite our prowess in the arts and sciences. Crises of identity lead often down the path of nationalism and worse. Since a national character cannot be politically manufactured, Tony Blair might be in for a hard ride in his quest for a 'New Britain'. Identity results from a shared history. It is not a Meccano set.

Those of my grandparents' generation were untroubled by such theoretical constructs. Their feet were on the ground, and the ground was pits or pots and a terrace a stone's throw from either. When I was young my

Tunstall grandmother recounted her memories of the town in mourning for
the death of Victoria. She had married my grandfather, she 18, he 14 years
her senior, and had scant knowledge of her roots. In a life lived for the day,
roots weren't as important as bread and dripping. It is only now, with the
easy availability of census returns and the microfiche, that I would have been
able to tell her she came from a family of Endon wheelwrights, and that her
own grandfather, Robert Brookes, came to Tunstall some time in the 1850s
to continue his trade where the clever money was. Her father John was born,
along with nine siblings, to a life of cramped hardship in a Wedgwood Street
back-to-back.

My father was one of seven children. Five survived. Robert died aged
two, of bronchial pneumonia, despite my grandmother's attempts at a cure
using steam from the range kettle. Doris was a year older. It is said she had
swallowed belladonna, attracted by the purple berries which hung in clusters
in the woods near their Longbridge Hayes home. My grandfather, orphaned
at 12, a collier at 13, continued at the face through the early years of his
marriage. When the family moved to Lime Street he made the six mile
journey to Chatterley Whitfield six days a week, usually on foot, occasionally
hitching a lift on a coal truck.

Harry Senior, my maternal grandfather, came from Yorkshire but settled
in London, where my mother was born. Like my Tunstall grandfather, he
came from humble stock. Unlike him, Harry opted for a life of adventure.
He ran away to sea just after his 13th birthday, serving his time on the
clippers leaving Tilbury docks. My mother was one of five children born to
him and his wife, Alice.

Shortly before my mother's arrival Harry landed a stoker's job on the
Titanic. He was a strong, thick-set man and survived the rigours of the
Atlantic. He told my mother he had to fight his way on to an already
overloaded boat before being rescued by the Carpathia and taken to New
York. He was one of the first to be interviewed. Two years later Harry was
again afloat, serving his time on the Q boats which defended the North
Atlantic convoys during the 1914-18 war.

Meanwhile, my Tunstall grandfather's brother George had joined the
queue at the local recruiting office and, together with grandmother's brother
Bob, opted to take the King's shilling. George came back an avowed
communist and a pacifist. Bob never came back. He died on the Somme and

is buried near Amiens. He was 21 when he died. My grandmother Ridgway, who passed away in 1977, never forgot the black-edged note her father received from the War Office.

My family were not immune to the slumps which came in the wake of peace. Those who worked in the pots were hit especially hard, though there were those who had done well out of the hostilities and who cast austerity aside to buy the products of the jazz age. Unsurprisingly, Clarice Cliff and the crudely bright designs which heralded the Art Deco era sold in London, not in Stoke.

My father was the victim of one of the frequent lay-offs in the tile factory where he worked. He got a more secure job as a policeman in the Met. By 1933 he had left his roots, the first member of his family to do so, and travelled to the 'heathen city' to face the unknown. He met my mother on his Deptford beat. Harry Senior died of cancer the year after they were married and two years later war was declared. My father was in a reserved occupation; his sisters in Stoke worked on munitions and my mother's brothers George and Harry were both called up. Harry followed his father into the Navy. George joined the army. I was born in the second year of the war. I remember searchlights, the drone of enemy bombers, the pin prick of lights in the night sky from the doorway of an air raid shelter, a half-flooded Anderson in the garden, barrage balloons tethered by the Thames and trips to the gate in my battered pedal car. Our street was bombed. The fireplace in my bedroom was blown from the wall and crushed the adjacent bed. I was told I slept through it. I don't remember anything of the incident, nor the day my father was buried under masonry as a VI exploded 100 yards from where he was walking. He told me what fear meant: a man trying to hide behind a single brick; an overweight woman leaping high into a steel tank; a bus climbing a wall; a school with children and staff alike laid blanketed on the playground; a stampede to reach the safety of the Underground, leaving many trampled underfoot.

All this my generation has been spared. Harry went down with the HMS Cornwall in the South China Sea. His brother George survived the Burma railway. I remember going to meet his ship at Liverpool in 1945. He weighed less than six stone when he came back. He told my mother that the best meal he had had in four years was a dog's leg.

Attlee's Labour government espoused the jubilation of a victorious nation. Drs Richmond and Halpin, our local practitioners, now worked for the newly created National Health Service. For the first time working people were free of the tyranny of ill health. Nor was a decent education the province of the few able to pay for it. The grammars were open to those of an academic bent, regardless of class or income. The new council estates boasted tree-lined streets and a garden front and back for every house. I was a beneficiary of all three, and grew up in that marvellous decade after the war where a quiet civility still existed but where the vibrancy of the 1960s was awaiting its turn on the stage. We thought we were tough and sophisticated, with our luminous socks, crepes and swept back hair. Looking back, we were still engagingly parochial, and there was little that Elvis, Little Richard and the rest could do about it.

Then the 1960s happened. Overnight, it seemed, potters were deserting the PMT and driving to work in their Ford Anglias. Television - everyone had bought one for the Queen's coronation a few years earlier - was in full swing along with The Beatles, Dr Who, the first American-inspired tower blocks and satellite towns. My father acquired an Austin. It had been converted from a van and usually broke down at weekends. A friend of mine dropped on a pre-war Standard and I bought an MG Midget for a few pounds. Now it would be worth a fortune.

My grandfather Ridgway died, aged 84. Grandma was to remain very much alive for some years, her longevity probably due to eating plenty of fat and abstaining from jogging in her youth. Lime Street, where she had lived most of her life, was cleared.

I married and moved into the countryside, where my children grew up with only anecdotal evidence of wars, slumps and the Draconian bosses of yesteryear. The kind of consumerism which began in earnest in the 1980s is a fact of life for them, as are the technological developments which render goods obsolescent before they have reached the end of the production line and make a new watch available for the price of a bunch of flowers. Even in my youth, a watch was a prized item.

The millennium is on us. The next century and those which follow will bring new problems. My grandfather believed that a meal on the table and a roof over his head was luck indeed. He lived through slumps and two world wars. My father was one of many whose lives were scarred by what they had suffered in the Second World War. I lived through a time of increasing plenty. I've never fired a gun in anger and I had a job for life. My children won't be so lucky.

What will the future hold? Inevitably, global business will grow, eclipsing national governments which will take on the sort of PR role Tony has with global trade. Opposing the power of the multinationals will be increasingly militant environmental and nationalistic movements. The growth in human population will reach crisis point. It will affect our children and possibly be responsible for mass starvation in the Third World unless the status of women in those countries most at risk can quickly be improved.

So we approach the millennium with hope tempered with caution. There will be mania and fireworks, yes. But will there be that jubilant fin de siecle mood enjoyed by the crowds in the last day of the 19th century, when science would surely provide a cure for every human ill and a sterile, science/business managed planet was not even a concept?

I sit on my balcony and watch the sun setting over Santorini. This is as good as it gets.

The Ridgway family line up by my grandparent's Lime Street house in 1945.
Grandma, Aunt Sib,Grandad, Aunt Dorothy, Dad, holding me, and Mum. Cousin Pat on sill.

2. A FIFTIES CHRISTMAS

I remember Christmas nights when I was young,
And sometimes, still, in dreams I seem to glide
Through streets of tinkling bells and ice-pebble stars.
The Man in the Moon is tethered to his tower,
And whispy deer
Scud with parcels through a sapphire sky.

Holding my mother's hand,
I walk beneath coloured lights
Which set the snow on fire,
The wine and whisky light of sweet shop windows,
And flickering flares
Which melt like icicles
In the ringing air.

I hear the hum of evening cars,
The slither of their tyres
In furrows of ice-water and half-melted snow,
See candle-light buses plodding through the dusk
And ice-cream taxis stiff with cold.

Up High Street we glide,
Bags bulging tinsel and magic painting books,
Tangerines in nets, twists of barley sugar
And chestnuts split for the hearth.
My bare knees smart,
My boots sink stud-deep in slush
And pattern my Burberry in icy flakes.
Gaudy rainbows dance before us,
Gift-burdened firs
Shoot emerald spears across the snow
And flashing baubles dance
From set to set
In an effort to keep pace.

Mallinder's radio
Carols a greeting to the tinsel-wrapped Raleighs,
Fizzing accumulators,
Boxed lamps, pumps and bells.
To holly-decked Danby's,
'Half a pound of brazils, Frank,
Give myself a treat.'
And Frank's chill-chapped fingers
Tap the till -
'A Merry Christmas
And remember me to Bill.'
The lights grow brighter
As we reach The Square,
Two worlds on either side the glass,
The Town Hall a silent umpire,
Blindly vigilant above the throng.

Into Woolworths,
Its glazed door proof against the cold,
But not the whisps
Swept in by feet
Eager for warmth and trinkets,
Old Betty Plants and cream whisks,
Crackers and party hats,
Miniature snowmen
In swirling worlds of their own,
Skipping ropes for the girls,
Gift-wrapped chocolates for nephews
And balsa monoplanes
With Instructions for Assembly
On a shelf behind.

The till clangs and for a moment
I glimpse wealth,
Silver sixpences, florins, half-crowns,
Thrupences of tarnished brass.

We turn into the Square,
The moon no longer tethered to the tower
But beaming at us
From the school in Forster Street.
Deer turn to Santa as I watch,
Hauling his cotton-wool beard
From here to Bradwell Wood
Until nothing remains
But a single, shrinking tuft.
In the Home and Colonial
Unseen hands whiz boxes through the air,
While snug in her wall-glazed office
The cashier beams an unassailable smile
And dreams of Christmas roast,
Lime Street, Jeff Chandler at the Ritz
And summers in Ilfracombe.
Strains of music creep under the door,
For the Salvation Army
Are God-resting gentlemen everywhere,
The gentleman and ladies
Stiffly-uniformed
And militarily capped,
Breathing incense into the charcoal night,
Their gloveless fingers stiff on the stops.
Horn, trumpet and trombone
Wink with coloured stars
As homeward-humming cars
Struggle through their notes.

The market is as numb as shodless feet.
The stone flags freeze
And echo to the called-out
Greetings of dark coated women
With hessian bags,
Wicker baskets, woolly mufflers
And wine-red faces flushed with cold.

The berried stalls are decorated
In baroque characters,
Arabesques and other motifs,
J. Podmore, merchant, A. Clowes and the rest,
Purveyors of this and that.
Agatha Christie Penguins for 6d,
Red rubber bones and brown rubber bands,
Calico bolts, ribbon and brocade,
Broken ginger-nuts,
Balloons and bars,
Zips and fasteners,
Joints of prime and poultry,
Toffee hammered to digestible chunks
And swung in grease-proof bags
Ready for extraction.

Into Station Road.
Slushy imprints turn to ice
Beneath Barber's Deco cloisters,
Silent, now,
No entrance token ringing
Or commissionaire barking
'Room for six at the back'
From the shelter of his
Epauletted coat.
'We Three Men' floating dimly from the Square,
Are laid to rest

By Arthur's ticking Bedford,
Its slat seats and trapped bags
Homely in the dark.
A penny buys a ticket,
Clipped from the range,
And a homeward ride.

Tomorrow I might pull my sledge
Up Hill Sixty,
Or Hill Forty Five,
Whatever the Christmas number,
Grease the runners with dripping,
Fling passengers into the powdered snow.
Now, home.
The wind plays tunes on the water pipes
And films the bedroom panes with ice.
But here the fire-shadows leap,
Orange imps rustle the coal
And flicker my childhood
Across the wall.

Now there are a thousand tinkling moons
In roof-tops everywhere
Waiting, like me,
For Christmas.

3. A SIXTIES CHRISTMAS

Autumn's memory
Trapped in the drawer for another year,
I'd don my Christmas Crimplenes
And drive heaterless through the murk.
I was Jack the Lad, Stirling Moss'd
Behind the wheel of my £50 sports car,
Torn hood,
Worn wood.
All the girls fancied me.

I'd linger in many a festive bar
Eyeing up the local talent,
Cilla Black bouffant, eye-liner
Black as a miner's hand.

Before The Day came
We'd be off to pubs decked in festive bunting,
The Mermaid with its bottomless pool,
The Wheatsheaf at Onneley,
The Cock Inn at Stableford
And others frequented by
Sophisticated habitues like me,
And gnarled septuagenarians
Who puffed their pipes
Behind the pickled eggs and talked farming
In slow, lazy tones
From the cramped security of the snug.

That was the Glorious Sixties, of course,
Before volumising hairspray,
Capped teeth,
Myopia
And trigger-finger set in.
At the Crystal I'd make my play,
Be an interesting bystander,
The strong, silent type
Whose magnetic charm
Demanded attention from the bar
And rarely got it.

Turned out for the Christmas special
In my see-through nylon shirt,
Rainbow socks, and terylene suit
Steaming from the last foxtrot,
I'd leer over my Worthington E
And assume a nonchalant cool,
Disregarded by the girls giggling past,
Hands forever fluttering
In minute sequinned bags
As the balloons come down.
What did they care for my
Six pack and Captain Marvel chest,
(With just a hint of hair)
Barnett black as a raven's wing
And eyes to put
Darcy to shame?

I attended many a Christmas party
At that time.
Clutching my Dave Brubeck LP,
A bag of booze to hand,
I climbed many a snowy path
And made drink-fuelled chat
With Brownhills' girls
Who exchanged bored glances
Over my shoulder
When they thought I wasn't looking.

I scraped the conversational barrel:
Profumo and Keeler,
JFK, Wily Mac and the Winds of Change,
Khrushchev and the Kinks,
Modern jazz, trad jazz, mainstream jazz
And all that jazz,
While the home-going snow flurried at the window
And draped my car in icy flakes.

But home was not for me -
Not yet at any rates.
I preferred the party spirit,
Snogging couples and smoochy dances,

Each spin of the record
Bringing fresh spats: Stones or Beatles?
Beach Boys or Baccarach?
Or an unattended silence
As the needle scratched its course?

Those were the days,
The sweater-clad '60s
Of Christmas innocence
And goodwill to everyone -
Even your ex-girlfriend's
Latest bloke.
Far from the Land of
Charcoal socks,
Urban blocks,
Sciatica,
Insomnia,
Dyspepsia,
Dyslexia,
Ethnicity,
Accountability,
And the Thirty Hour Day.
My childhood '50s
Far behind,
The ancient Bush churning out
Donald Peers and the rest,
The second-hand Raleigh
Wheeled past the banister
And propped by the bedroom wall,
Rupert Bear and magic painting books
With pictures of wrecked galleons
Forgotten.

My Sixties Christmases a much grander affair,
The products more dynamic.
Now I awoke to a Pifco trouser press,
A Hardy Amies shirt,
A foot pump and various other accessories

Dumped by the fairy
At the foot of the bed.
I can vouch for this
Elasticity of time.
I am my parents
Four decades on.
No stolen mistletoe kiss now,
No joke binoculars
Passed around at party-time
To blacken the unwary eye.
No draughty MG, dodgy wipers
Fighting the snow.
And Jack the Lad
Long since settled for slippers
And a mug of Bovril.

But in the mood
I can still revive those distant dreams,
Give them artificial respiration
And watch them grow.
See anew the mini-skirted girls,
Suited boys,
Opaque Christmas fogs and dusky snow,
Hear occasional carols
And, later, welcome the New Year
With a lump of coal from
Somewhere around the back.

Happy times
Made happier by recollection,
Gathering dust in an attic box
Labelled Christmas Past.

But this
Christmas Now
Is downstairs still -
At least until it's over.

'Almost on my doorstep': Chatterly Whitfield Colliery.

4. THE WATCH

The flat was nothing to write home about but it was all we could afford at the time. It was all due to rationalisation - which is a fancy way of saying I got the push along with 200 others.

The first to go was the house. We had to sell up and take what we could. I was even lucky to get the flat. Three rooms over a newsagent's with a shared loo and yobs doing wheelies by the wall at night. Still, that's all behind us now. I suppose you could say we're on our feet again.

My wife, Pam, supported me through the hard times. I don't know how she put up with it. If it had been me I think I would have walked out. Not Pam. When the black moods came, she bucked me up. When we were scraping the barrel, she always managed to make ends meet. When I had bad dreams it was Pam who calmed me down.

But not even Pam could explain the watch. I've still got it in my drawer and every so often I take it out and sit staring at it, wondering how on earth I came to have it. I'm no nearer an answer now than I was 18 years ago, when I came back from Chatterley Whitfield Colliery through the snow and fell onto my bed, exhausted.

But I need to go back. Redundancy affected me badly. I began to have nightmares. I spent my dreams with all sorts of strange, distorted faces from the past. The doctor prescribed some pills, but they only made things worse. And one of the dreams I shall never forget. Not only because of its intensity, but because the experience was directly linked to the old pocket-watch I'm looking at now.

I remember the date for a reason I'll give later. February 7, 1981. I'd spent an hour hoping for sleep, and by the time I turned off the lamp Pam was spark out. I must have dozed off shortly after.

The next thing I knew, I was sitting bolt upright. I could hear voices in the street and my first thought was the local kids were playing up again. I parted the curtains and looked out. It was unnaturally quiet. Maybe it was the muffling effect of the snow. It had already settled on the road and was building up in the lower corners of the window. It was a view I'd had plenty of time to study before, but now things seemed different.

It could have been a trick of the light, but the grassed-over slag heap seemed lower. And lights were twinkling in the old colliery buildings. There was something else, too. As I stood there, I could swear I heard the dim clanking of wagons. I thought my mind was playing games. I decided to make a cup of tea and I'd just turned from the window when voices rose again from below.

This time I saw where they were coming from - a group of half a dozen men. They were running across the allotments towards the colliery. I had no time to wonder what they'd been up to before I heard a loud banging on the downstairs door. I always kept a stick handy by the bed. I decided now might be the time to use it. I opened the door, ready with the shillelagh. Instead of the yob I expected, a middle-aged man stood there. He wore a cap and muffler and looked as nervous as a greyhound. I opened my mouth to ask him what the hell he wanted at that time of night when he grabbed the pocket of my dressing gown.

"Th' pit's in trouble. Cum on."

I stared into his thin, shadowed face. I could make no sense of it. "Tha's got a pair of 'ands, 'asna? Get thee rags on and get up t' bank."

He went next door with the same message. Now the street echoed to the sound of men's voices. I found myself getting dressed. I left Pam asleep and went out.

It was bitterly cold. Snow stung my face and biting gusts whipped dust from the shale banks. Everyone was running towards the pit. As I stumbled over sleepers and dirt I could hear a distant commotion. It took me 10 minutes before I reached the first of the colliery buildings. At least a hundred people were gathered in the weak light. Most were men, but there were some women, too, shawled against the night.

Some way ahead there was frenzied activity. Half a dozen men were leading ponies into a nearby paddock. They weren't moving fast enough for one man. As I watched he aimed a kick at one of the animals and gave vent to a stream of invective, though I was too far away to pick up much of what he said. I looked around at the huddled figures in the yard. No one spoke, no one moved. Every face was turned towards the pit head, faintly visible through the snowy squalls.

I felt isolated. I was involved in something I couldn't understand, but at the same time I was remote from it. Then a gust of wind brought an acrid stench of smoke and a dull roar rose from the crowd.

"Th' Institute's afire," someone shouted, pointing towards the billowing wreaths.

Then a woman's distraught voice pierced the growing clamour. "Our Eddie's down there. God 'elp us."

Other women gathered around, disconsolate as herself. The crowd's mood was turning bellicose, their pent-up frustration giving vent to angry oaths. I heard the name Thompson spoken dismissively within earshot.

Then heads turned as a lamp-lit britska moved fast through the crowd. Someone said it was Atherton, the old colliery manager. It stopped far up by the colliery buildings and the man who had kicked out at the pony went over to him.

"We want five men to go below." His voice rose thinly through the air. "Volunteers up here, now." I felt a hand on my shoulder and turned. The man who had knocked me up was pushing forward with me in tow. "Tha doesna' want be hanging out with th' women, dust? Come. Let's give Thompson a 'and."

I joined the group at the pit head. Despite his blackened face, I recognised signs of panic on Thompson's features. He caught his breath and struggled to control himself.

"What d'yer want us do, Mr Thompson?' one of the volunteers asked.

"Do? What dust think ah want thee do? Ah want th' rest o' th'osses brought up.

"Th'osses, Mr Thompson? What about the men?"

"Ar't questionin' my orders?"

"Nay, thar't th' manager."

"Mak' certain tha knows it. Atherton can come down an' all. And ma two lads."

We began to trail after him. The air was thick with smuts. Dark tendrils rose from the Institute shaft and trailed across the waste. We turned by the winding house. The pithead gear climbed into the darkness. Below it the cage waited.

Thompson stepped into it, Atherton following with one of Thompson's sons. I caught his words: "Come next week and we'll 'ave that smithy moved up top, Father." He might have begun to say something else. I don't know, for at that moment an ominous growl came from deep within the earth. I remember an eruption of flame and the ground beneath my feet seemed to give way. I had a sensation, no more than that, of the cage hurtling violently upwards......

I don't know how long I lay there. It could have been hours, though it was more likely seconds. I opened my eyes to see the cage crushed against the remains of the head gear.

There was a sound of running feet, and I saw a figure lying a short way off. People were shouting: "It's young Thompson." I managed to struggle to my feet and went over to where he lay. He was a mess. The fingers of his left hand were clasped around something.

Help arrived and he was wrapped up and stretchered away. I watched them vaguely through the snow. Then I saw what it was he had been holding. It must have dropped from his fingers as they lifted him up. It was a watch, a hunter with a length of broken chain.

I brushed the snow from its face. Miraculously it was still ticking. The fingers read 3.15. I felt a hand on my shoulder and turned blankly.

"Are yer all right?" asked a voice.

"Ah think so."

"'ere, 'ave a sup o' this." The man put a bottle to my lips. I took a mouthful and pushed it away. "Ah don't need that. Ah'll be better for a walk."

I left him capping his whisky and set off for home. I heard a woman crying faintly, but the crowds were as insubstantial as shadows and I found myself at the front door without knowing how I had got there. I remember the stairs, the patter of sleet against the panes and Pam still asleep with her face to the wall. Flashes of light played behind the curtains. Then I awoke.

It was daylight. Pam was standing by the bed. She handed me a mug. I sat up and took a sip.

"I've just been having one of my dreams," I said.

"What happened?"

"There was a fire at the pit."

I could see the grassed over mound from where I lay, propped up on a pillow. "It was so real I can't believe it didn't happen."

She sat on the bed. "You were up in the night. Sleep-walking."

"Sleep-walking?"

"I woke up myself at half past three. The bed was cold. You were standing by the window dressed in your old clothes."

"What was I doing?"

"Just looking." She put her hand in her jeans pocket and took out the watch. "I found this in your jacket. Where's it from?"

***

I thought there must be a simple explanation. I have tried to convince myself of it for 18 years without success. Then last week I went to Hanley to do some Christmas shopping. It couldn't be avoided - I have three grandchildren now - though I am not partial to the crowds, I must admit.

I thought I might get something to read for the youngest, and found myself in a bookshop for the first time in years. I found what I wanted - one of those pop-up picture books small kids like - when for some reason the 'Local' section caught my eye. I had an hour to kill, and found myself browsing through the shelves. Jammed between two volumes was a slim book: North Staffordshire Pit Disasters.

A tremor ran through me. I steadied myself and began to read about the underground smithy that set fire to the pit. About the explosion. About Edward Thompson, the manager of Chatterley Whitfield Colliery, and Atherton his predecessor. About the 24 men who had died. It happened on February 7, 1881. I had had my dream on the same date - a century later.

So what can I add? It's something you don't like to talk about. But I know. And Pam, of course. And we still have the watch. Edward Thompson's son, John, didn't survive. He was in no state to worry where his watch had got to. So let's just say I'm keeping it safe for a while.

'...looking towards the kilns with their cargo of glowing bricks':
The brickworks and marl hole at Berry Hill Colliery.

5. THE LAST FIRING

The ground between the kilns had been churned to an icy slurry by the iron-rimmed wheels. The barrowmen had worked under lowering winter clouds, carting loads of red brick from the drying sheds to the oven placers in teams of three. By the time the kiln was closed the first heavy flakes were falling.

Jud Kelsall stood for moment at his window. The sets gleamed treacherously in the lamplight, and a thin sheet had already whitened the pavement. He didn't want to go. He didn't feel up to it. A sense of foreboding seemed to hover in the chill parlour air. He shook himself free of his oppressive mood, pulled his cap over his eyes and jerked at his muffler. He *had* to go. One more shift, one more pay packet. The last payment on the house. Then it would be his. His daughter stood in the doorway.

"Yer've forgotten summat."

He turned, quizzically.

"Yer snappin'. My, it's come to a pretty pass if yer forgettin' th' most important thing."

She stood by him and looked up at the sky. "Looks as if there's more where that came from. Just watch yer footin' down th' riggot, feyther. It'll be like a sheet of ice down there."

He opened the door. A flurry blew across the dresser. He turned to his daughter. "Th' last firing, Mary."

"Whatever do yer mean?"

"It's takken me 30 years t' pay for this roof. One last firing and it's mine. And when I go, it'll be thine."

She lifted her hand involuntarily to her cheek. "Go on with yer, you and yer last firing. Yer'd 'ave nowt do if yer weren't feedin' them ovens."

A shard path dropped between high, derelict walls to the brickyard. The kilns loomed out of the darkness as he drew near. By the far kiln he could hear the noise of shovelled coal. A single firemouth glowed red. Apart from this and a weak oil lamp above the office building, the bank was in darkness.

Jud felt Harris's eyes on him as he clocked on. Harris was the foreman, a thick-jowled braggart who spent his time carrying tittle-tattle upstairs when he wasn't laying men off.

"And 'ow's th' fireman ternayght?"

Jud made no reply. "Tha's best get them ovens stoked. And 'ave thee wits about thee. Mind tha's only paid good from kiln."

"Tha'll be tellin' me summat I dunna know next," Jud said. It was the practice to withhold payment from the men if any of the bricks in the kiln were ruined. It was Jud's job to make sure the firing ensured a perfect batch.

Jud went out to the kilns. The snow was coming thicker now. A dangerous deposit was building up along the paths. He instructed the men to shovel the burning coals from the single lit firemouth into the other firemouths as firing commenced. Six ruby dots of flame now lit the first kiln, and a thin wreath of smoke rose into the night. "Tha' canst begin baitin'," Jud told the men. "And go careful. Yer don't want t' put 'em out."

More coal was applied to each fire. Jud adjusted the growing flames with long-practised ease, working the pulleys which controlled the dampers with the delicacy of an artist. *Keep the temperature low at first. Drive the moisture from the brick. Not enough to bend or distort or discolour. Then a gradual build-up to firing. The last firing. Take account of the wind, the snow, the season, of Harris and of "good from the kiln." One last firing, one perfect batch and the house will be hers.*

He worked steadily into the early hours. The kiln's warmth made a nimbus of slush in the snow. Despite the cold, the men had discarded their jackets. Jud gave instructions to begin firing the second kiln. But he was working slower than usual, and there was a drowsy aching in his joints. He fought for breath, leaned against the wall of the wage office to recoup his strength. He would normally stay at the kilns for a couple of days until the firing cycle was complete, snatching a nap where he could after giving the men their instructions. But he had to have rest. He had to get home.

At five in the morning his shift ended. He called over one of the men. "Ah'm 'avin' t' leave th' bank, Jack. Ah'm not feelin' reyght. Tha' knows what t' do. Ah'll be back ternayght. It'll be plenty o' time afore soakin' in this weather." Jack nodded. "Soaking" was when the oven had reached maximum temperature. This would be held for three hours as the bricks hardened.

"At sure, Jud? Dust want me get Charlie in? 'e'll do relief if yer like."

"Ah'll be back at nine sharp. No need fer reliefs."

He stood in the parlour dark, wretched, with barely enough strength to take off his cap and boots. Mary and her son were still in bed. He struggled up the staircase and fell on to the bed.

By one Mary grew anxious and went upstairs. She found him swathed in blankets and deathly pale. A sudden panic seized her and she shook him awake. He regarded her with feverish eyes. "Aren't yer feelin' well, feyther? What's wrong?"

He gripped her wrist. His coarse palms abraded her skin. "Mary, tha' mustna forget. After ternayght th' ouse is thine. It's thine and young Mark's. Dunna forget. After this last....." His voice began to falter. "It's th' last firin'.... like ah told thee....

"Yer talkin' nonsense, feyther. Yer t' stay in bed. Ah'll get th'doctor up. Mark can go down th' yard, tell 'em t' get the relief in."

He restrained her with a weak hand. "They'll get th' relief in without your say-so if 'e's needed. 'e won't be needed. Ah'll be down ternayght as usual. They wunna know what t' do less ah show 'em."

The doctor diagnosed exhaustion. On no account was she to let him through the door. Complete rest. Rest and beef stock. Rest and warmth.

Night came. The firemouths glowed crimson, and bands of ochre smoke met the pall of cloud. The boy stoking a fire felt a sudden chill, and turned abruptly. Jud stood there, watching him, saying nothing.

"Ah was just tendin' th' oven, Mr Kelsall." Jud looked on without speaking. The boy continued on the far side of the kiln. Jack came up.

"So tha's made it after all, Jud. Are we on top o' th' job?"

Jud bent to a spy hole. A fiery yellow band glinted in his eyes. He turned to Jack and smiled. Jack smiled back. "We'll do a trial," Jud said.

Jack thought the fireman's voice had lost something of its firmness. It seemed to come from far away. "Ah'll tak out the ring, Jack. Ah'll do a trial."

Jud withdrew a Buller's ring from the kiln and examined it without comment. He sighed. The brightness of the ring cast a ribbon across his body. For a moment it seemed to shine through him. He put it back.

"Best open th' dampers round this side. We're nearly up to temperature. We're nearly there."

Jud slowly manipulated the pulleys. Flames gushed upwards. A trail of smoke underbellied the low cloud. Jack looked over to where Jud had been and caught sight of him by the far oven. He had his jacket on again. And his mufffler. He was just standing, standing still, looking towards the kilns with their cargo of glowing bricks.

"Jud? Is summat up?"

Jud made no move. The fireglow burnished his face and body in a halo of light. He was unusually distinct in the darkened yard. "Tha canst let th' fires out now. It's all done. The last.... ay, the very last firin'." His voice was a distant monotone. Jack turned to the kiln, a boy with him. One by one they began to close the dampers.

***

Mary's ears pricked up. It was five in the morning. She had been unable to sleep. She sat up, listening intently. It was her father. Even on the snow-muffled street she could recognise his gait. She waited for the door to grate and close, and the interval that would elapse before the stairs began to creak. She heard him on the first step. But what was he doing, going to work after what the doctor had said? He hadn't the strength to leave his bed. When she'd gone to bed herself, she'd put her nose around his door. He'd been swaddled like an infant.

"Feyther!" she called. "Is that you?" There was no reply. She left her bed, threw a wrap around her shoulders and crossed the landing. Jud's room was in darkness. There was no sound. She lit a candle and brought the flame down to the fireman's sleeping face. The shock made her cry out.

Later that morning, when the wages had been made up, one of the lads from the brickyard called at the house. He found the parlour curtains drawn. He knocked and waited for Jud. But Mary stood there instead. Her face was the texture of Parian. Her blue-ringed eyes had a haunted look.

"Mr 'arris 'as sent me with Mr Kelsall's wages. 'e says all th' bricks were good from th' oven. 'e says t' tell Mr Kelsall 'e needn't bother commin termorrer as 'e's layin' off."

Mary didn't seem to hear. The boy waited on the step. Still not looking at the envelope, she reached out her hand for it. "Jud was down the yard all last night, was he?"

"Ay, Missus. Like 'e always is."

"And all th' bricks got fired?"

"Ay, like they always are."

She brought her eyes up until they rested levelly on the boy's.

"Yer mun do me a favour. Tell Mr 'arris it doesn't matter much t' me feyther whether 'e's laid off or not. Tha' mun tell Mr 'arris ah've just 'ad th' doctor up. 'e says me feyther's bin dead these 12 hours."